ALSO BY THE AUTHORS

Humanize

When Millennials Take Over

The **NON-OBVIOUS GUIDE TO**

Employee Engagement

(For Millennials, Boomers & Everyone Else)

By **MADDIE GRANT AND JAMIE NOTTER**

IDEAPRESS
PUBLISHING

IDEAPRESS
PUBLISHING

Published in the United States by Ideapress Publishing.

IDEAPRESS PUBLISHING | WWW.IDEAPRESSPUBLISHING.COM

All trademarks are the property of their respective companies.

COVER DESIGN BY JOCELYN MANDRYK

Cataloging-in-Publication Data is on file with the Library of Congress.
ISBN: 978-1940858746

SPECIAL SALES

Ideapress Books are available at a special discount for bulk purchases
for sales promotions and premiums, or for use in corporate training
programs. Special editions, including personalized covers, a custom
foreword, corporate imprints and bonus content are also available.

Non-Obvious® is a registered trademark of the Influential
Marketing Group.

DEDICATION

To all those who believe, like we do,
that work does not need to suck.

Read this book to understand why common employee engagement efforts aren't working. When you shift your thinking, and then arm yourself with the practical solutions in this book, you'll achieve results you never imagined could be possible.

Is This Guide for You?

If you picked up this book, you are not a dummy.

Many business guides treat you like an idiot. Some even say so on the cover. This is not one of those books.

The **Non-Obvious Guides** all focus on sharing advice that you haven't heard before. In this guide, you will learn all about what it takes to keep your best people engaged and inspire them to do their best.

I first worked with Maddie and Jamie on their book *When Millennials Take Over* and have been continually impressed with their ability to uncover exactly what it takes to help organizations attain the type of culture they have always wanted.

I know they both would love to share some of these insights over coffee with you. Until they get that chance, we all hope this book will be the next best thing!

Rohit Bhargava
Founder, *Non-Obvious Guides*

How to Read This Book

Throughout this book you will find links to helpful guides and resources online. Here is the URL where you can find all of these materials:

https://humanworkplaces.net/nonobvious-resources/

These symbols refer to content that will further your learning:

 → **TEMPLATES:**
Custom templates you can use for your own organization.

 → **DOWNLOADS:**
Useful further reading.

 → **TUTORIALS:**
Lessons and courses from our training site CultureCampus.net.

 → **VIDEOS:**
Short online videos with more information on a particular topic.

 → **AUDIO:**
Podcast episodes with more information on a particular topic.

 → **FURTHER READING:**
A note about a particularly relevant book related to the topic.

 → **CHAPTER SUMMARY:**
Quick takeaways and important points.

In this book, you will learn ...

→ How to define employee engagement in a way that connects directly to what makes both your organization and your employees more successful.

→ Why engagement surveys are so flawed and how to dig into your culture to go beyond "symptom" metrics.

→ When to let those Millennials (and others for that matter) hop to a new job after two years, and when to fight hard to keep them.

→ Why culture is more important than engagement and what the relationship is between the two.

→ Real, proven, and actionable advice on how to actually improve engagement.

→ How to drive engagement even if you're not "in charge of" engagement at your company.

Why We Wrote This Book

We wrote this book because we want the world of work to suck less.

That has been our joint passion for ten years now. Back in 2008, we were both consultants, tackling issues in the workplace from slightly different angles: Jamie's background in conflict resolution and organization development had him doing lots of staff retreats and facilitating problem solving sessions, and Maddie's expertise focused on the then nascent fields of digital strategy and building online communities.

But we quickly realized that in the end, we were both doing the same thing: helping organizations deal with culture change. So we started to speak and write about it. Our first co-authored book came out in late 2011, and it was titled *Humanize: How People-Centric Organizations Succeed in a Social World*. In it, we argued that social media was not just changing the way we market and communicate—it was changing the way we lead and manage. The cultural implications of the digital world were shifting cultures away from traditional management, which comes from an engineering mindset, where organizations are treated like machines, and towards a more human approach to organizations that value being open, trustworthy, generative, and courageous.

One of the unexpected benefits of writing *Humanize* is that it put us in touch with a growing community of leaders who were already embracing what we had been writing about with concrete actions. They had built organizations that we thought represented what the future of work would look like, and they were doing it today. That sparked the idea for our second book, *When Millennials Take Over: Preparing for the Ridiculously Optimistic Future of Business,* an Ideapress release in early 2015.

Building off of generational research we'd been doing for years, the book looks at the future of business through a Millennial lens, and then dives deep into four case studies from organizations who are making significant strides in aligning with those trends. We focus on four key capacities that businesses need in this Millennial era: to be digital, clear, fluid, and fast. The way to infuse this into your culture is through plays that drive success on an individual and organizational level.

That became our focus after the book was launched: helping people build cultures that made more sense in the Millennial era. We created a culture assessment called the Workplace Genome, and started consulting with companies at aligning their culture with what makes them successful in order to drive engagement.

And employee engagement, quite frankly, is in desperate need of some help. Every year we invest nearly $1 billion in improving engagement, yet we have no measurable results to show for it. After a decade of that lousy track record, we figured employee engagement was more than ripe for some non-obvious solutions.

We wrote this book with action in mind. We want to redefine employee engagement in a way that makes it easier to work with.

We provide a model for improving engagement that lends itself to immediate action. We give you several chapters of concrete examples of how to improve both culture and engagement—through technology, processes, and design—that drive success for your employees and organization.

The next step is yours! Read this book and start improving engagement today.

CHAPTER 1

What Employee Engagement Really Is

By now you've likely seen the frightening statistics about the lack of employee engagement in the American workforce (Gallup, State of the American Workplace 2017):

→ Only 33% of employees are considered engaged at work.

→ Nearly 20% are "actively disengaged," meaning they are intentionally sabotaging the organizations for which they work.

Disengagement costs us $500 billion annually in lost productivity and turnover costs.[1]

Sounds horrible, doesn't it? And even worse, the statistics are probably in line with your own personal experiences in the workplace. You can picture them— the people you've worked with (and for) over the years that seemed to be just punching the clock, doing the bare minimum, frequently calling in "sick" on Fridays, and continuously complaining about their situation (yet doing nothing to improve it).

And sure, you can also picture your highly engaged colleagues—positive attitude, consistently going above and beyond the call of duty, coming up with new solutions to every challenge thrown at them, and actively mentoring others internally. But we're betting you can think of more disengaged colleagues in your past than the engaged ones.

The "Crisis" of Disengagement

If you believe the statistics, then we've got a ten-cylinder car, but only three of the cylinders are really working to full spec, and two of the cylinders are not only immobile—they're oozing some sort of sludge that is slowly ruining the rest of the engine. We bought a Ferrari, and it's running like a Yugo. This would explain why organizations in the U.S. are spending close to a whopping $1 billion every year trying to solve the employee engagement crisis. Imagine the productivity and effectiveness we could tap into if we could only access the power of those other seven cylinders. We'd finally get our Ferrari!

Not so fast. Despite the multi-billion-dollar investment, we are not seeing real results. The mainstream measures of engagement in the past several years have shown minimal to no increase in the engagement levels in the U.S. workforce. Some have shown an actual decline. How is this possible?

While employee engagement DOES matter, we have been completely misunderstanding it. The crisis we have is not actually the crisis we think we have.

The Real Meaning of Employee Engagement

There are a lot of definitions of employee engagement out there, and they're all missing the mark. It's not that they are inaccurate—it's that the way we define engagement is making it harder, ironically, for us to solve the problem of disengagement. Here's what's happening:

Engagement is most commonly defined as the level of "emotional commitment or connection" an employee has to the organization and its goals. That's an intuitively satisfying definition. We can certainly imagine someone who is committed and connected working very hard and giving extra effort. It makes sense.

There is no direct method to improve someone else's level of emotional connection and commitment.

It's internal. You can't make someone love you. Despite this fact, there is currently a $1 billion industry trying to help companies make this happen anyway.

Researchers and consultants have been making cases for their particular models for moving the needle on engagement, which includes things like having a best friend at work, getting consistent feedback from managers, creating a clear career path, etc.

The research has been mostly correlational—for example, the highly engaged employees tend to report more often that they get a lot of feedback from managers (i.e., feedback and engagement are positively correlated). Seeing that correlation, we assume that giving people feedback is a solution to the engagement problem—it will improve that level of emotional commitment and connection.

Except sometimes it doesn't. Sometimes, we give them more feedback and it has zero impact on their level of engagement. That's the problem with correlations.

We haven't necessarily identified the underlying cause, which is why we're not moving the collective needle on engagement.

We're chasing solutions based on correlations and not understanding the root cause at all. That $1 billion investment is focused on the symptoms, and it's not working.

We are suggesting a more direct approach. Let's define engagement in a way that identifies root causes up front:

Story: **QUALITY LIVING INCORPORATED**

Quality Living, Incorporated (QLI) is a company in Omaha, Nebraska that provides rehabilitation services to individuals with brain and spinal cord injuries. We chose them as a case study for our previous book, *When Millennials Take Over,* because they are a great example of an organization that embraced one of the four "future of work" capacities we identified in our research: Fluid (i.e., flexible hierarchy).

Employee engagement levels in this company are through the roof. They have won the "best place to work" award so many times in their market that the contest organizers had to create a special category for them—just so others would have a chance to win.[2] They have different metrics for positive turnover (people who are low performers or a bad fit for the culture) and negative turnover (people they wanted to stay, but left anyway), and their negative turnover is always less than 10%, which is remarkable in the healthcare industry, where turnover is closer to 20%.

Their Employee Net Promoter score is +81 (ridiculously high, as you will learn later in this book). We've been to their campus— you can see it, feel it, hear it. People love working there.

How do they do it? By focusing rigorously on enabling employees to be successful.

As mentioned above, QLI is highlighted here because of its "fluid" or flexible hierarchy. While it has a fairly traditional organizational structure (CEO, VPs, directors, etc.), the way they live this hierarchy is different than most organizations we've come across. People at very low levels in the hierarchy have been known to lead meetings and make important decisions, while people at the highest levels will frequently hold back and defer to their colleagues in meetings. But this flexibility is not random. It is based specifically on what drives their success.

Remember that they are doing incredibly difficult work there—teaching people to walk again, or to speak again. In their words, they are "rebuilding shattered lives." To be successful in that endeavor, they realized early on that the healthcare solutions they are deploying (physical therapy, speech therapy, etc.) are more effective when they are connected to something deep inside the patient—hopes, dreams, aspirations. They need that emotional connection for the therapy to take hold within the patient.

With that success driver in mind, they run their meetings differently than many other organizations.

The most important person in the room is the one who knows the most about the hopes, dreams, and aspirations of the patient (regardless of their position in the hierarchy).

As one employee said, "There are no lines we can't cross in terms of creativity and what we can do for our residents."

To be clear, however, we're not arguing that decentralization is the key to engagement.

QLI didn't choose this flexible hierarchy because it sounds cool or they thought it would bump their engagement numbers. They chose it because it leads directly to their patients receiving more effective care and it empowers employees to be successful.

These are the kinds of efforts and organizational shifts that align individual and organizational success and really move the needle on engagement.

The Secret to Improving Engagement

Odds are, your engagement isn't as high as QLI's, but don't let that get you down. The whole point of this book is to help you with that.

So, here's the secret to improving engagement: Understanding your workplace culture.

We'll dig into culture more fully in Chapter 3, but here's the basic point: Your workplace culture communicates what is valued in your organization to everyone who works there, which will then drive their behavior.

If your culture ends up driving behaviors that do not drive (or even inhibit) their success, then your engagement will go down. But if you can intentionally shape your culture so it more consistently supports behaviors that align employee and organizational success, then you can have a huge impact on employee engagement.

Take a hard look at your culture. Is "the way we do things around here" messing with success? Maybe it's the way you distribute power internally that prevents people from being as agile as they need to be. Maybe you only talk the talk about innovation in your

CULTURE 101:

A brief course about how to define your culture and understand culture change.

culture, but have failed to put in place the right kinds of processes that will enable effective prototyping and experimentation among your employees, which makes it more difficult for your employees to deliver on what they promise. Maybe your strong silo walls prevent people from solving problems quickly and effectively, which adversely affects performance.

To improve engagement, you need to focus on the building blocks of your culture—the structures, processes, approaches, and priorities—and how they are either helping or hindering your people from performing successfully for themselves AND the enterprise.

Does that mean engagement will improve if you fix silos, innovation, and agility? Sort of—as long as you can tie those interventions directly to what makes people successful in your organizational context. When culture is aligned with success, you'll get your engagement.

Aren't the Millennials Changing Everything?

Since we're talking about organizational structures, processes, and culture, we have to address the generational issue. The Millennial generation (currently ranging in age from late teens to mid-thirties) has had a large impact on the workplace, both due to its size (it is the largest generation in U.S. history) and its different approach to work. As soon as Millennials started hitting the workforce in significant numbers ten or fifteen years ago, they started getting a lot of attention. Most of the attention has been quite negative, of course— they're entitled, too informal, don't know how to talk to people without using emojis, etc. We have been doing lots of fist-shaking about the "kids these days" and how they need to change. But frankly, that whole conversation is a waste of time. We call it the "discourse of complaining," and it needs to stop.

The Millennials are doing what every generation before them has done—they grew up in a distinct time period, and what was going on around them in society ended up shaping their values, approaches, and (more importantly for this discussion) behaviors in the workplace. Millennials grew up with the immense power and reach that comes with the internet, for example, so they're showing up in the workplace expecting to do more, faster, even as entry level employees. Fine. Gen X showed up with some cynicism and challenges with traditional hierarchy. Boomers showed up with an idealistic focus on teamwork and collaboration.

VISIT ONLINE RESOURCES FOR:

Abstract and sample chapter, *When Millennials Take Over* (2015)

Every generation has its "thing" and every generation pushed the envelope in the workplace when they got there. We don't need to freak out about it.

We've written a lot about generational differences in the workplace, so if you want to read more about this, please see the Appendix where we've included a summary, as well as the resource below.

But there is one factor that makes the entrance of the Millennials into the workforce more significant to the conversation about employee engagement (and workplace culture).

The Millennials are hitting the scene at the same time that leadership and management are changing radically.

With all the attention on how the Millennials are changing things in the workplace (and they are), we have almost overlooked the even bigger changes that are happening. We cover the evidence for that in much more detail in our previous book, *When Millennials Take Over: Preparing for the Ridiculously Optimistic Future of Business,* but here's the short version. There is an alignment between the way the Millennials are viewing leadership and management, and the way cutting-edge companies are breaking the rules of traditional management. And we don't mean "cutting-edge" as in the cool technology companies that are featured on the news (our case studies include a small nonprofit and a regional bank). We mean companies that are doing management differently and succeeding wildly in the process. We call them "positive deviants," and they are embracing a new approach to leadership that emphasizes things like transparency, decentralization, agility, speed, and flexibility, and at the same time they are running circles around the competition and have incredibly high engagement (like QLI, mentioned above). These companies (and the Millennials, for that matter) are shining a light on what we and a host of other pundits are calling the "future of work."

So what does all that have to do with engagement? The rules for running organizations are changing.

We're seeing more organizations coming up with different ways to align the success of their individual employees with the success of the organization, which is at the heart of engagement.

And since the Millennials are already moving in the direction of these changes (and there are 100 million of them), we should take the opportunity to learn from them as we move our organizations forward. That is why we will be discussing the Millennial impact on engagement throughout the book.

Now that we have a clearer understanding of the root cause of engagement (aligning individual and organizational success), in the next chapter we will look at where many organizations start: measuring engagement. Unfortunately, they are wasting a lot of time and money. Why? That's next.

**CHAPTER SUMMARY:
THREE THINGS TO REMEMBER**

→ We've been defining engagement wrong, making it impossible to actually move the needle on disengagement.

→ We need to create systems that address the root cause of engagement (or disengagement), by consistently enabling more individual AND organizational success.

→ A better understanding of culture is the secret to improving engagement.

CHAPTER 2

How to Start Measuring the Right Things

There is a problem with how we typically measure engagement and it starts at the very beginning with surveys.

Current engagement surveys measure symptoms or results—how people FEEL about the workplace. Those metrics are then used to fix the symptoms, without fully understanding the root causes. As a result, engagement scores go down, yet the next year we run the same process again, hoping for better results. This is the definition of insanity.

It's like taking your temperature. If the result is 98.6 degrees Fahrenheit, then you know you're on track, but if it's 101.5, you know there is a problem. The fever, however, is just an indicator. It is being caused by something, and the symptom metric does not really tell you enough about the cause. You'll need to look at other kinds of symptoms and gather and analyze completely different data to uncover the root cause (virus?

bacteria?), and then you will design interventions to deal with that cause, which will then move the body temperature (the symptom metric) back to normal. Fix the cause, and the symptoms improve.

Yet that is not how most organizations tackle the engagement problem.

Instead of collecting data to identify root causes, most organizations simply expand the data they collect on the symptoms, which then limits their solutions only to those symptoms.

They ask more and more questions in the survey every year:

→ Do you get feedback from your manager?

→ Are you happy?

→ Do you like the benefits?

→ Are you growing professionally?

→ Do your personal values align with the company values?

When any scores come back "unfavorable," they deploy solutions—change the benefits package, make managers give more feedback, fund more happy hours. Those are all lovely, but here's what happens: Next year, the engagement survey is still negative. It's like you took some ibuprofen to make the fever go down a bit, but you didn't kill the bacteria, so the fever comes back. Here's what you're missing:

The source of engagement is the alignment of individual and organizational success. "Symptom metrics" rarely measure that.

Instead of making your symptom metrics more complicated, you should simplify those, and then double down on measuring and understanding the root cause(s).

 ## The Ultimate Question for Employee Engagement

The purpose of measuring a symptom is that it will prompt you to take further action to address the cause. It's an alarm bell. It jolts you into action, though it won't tell you specifically what to do. So, don't develop engagement metrics (which are symptom metrics) that take three months to deploy and six months to analyze. Make them instant, and make them leading indicators, rather than lagging (i.e., they show up before things get really bad).

Asking your people if they have a best friend at work and a dozen other questions is not the way to go. Here's our alternative: Ask only one question.

How likely are you to recommend a friend/ colleague for employment here?

Have them answer on a scale from 0 to 10, and then use the Net Promoter Score (NPS) methodology to provide the results.[3] The Net Promoter method divides answers to that question into three categories:

→ **"Promoters" score a 9 or 10.** These are people who not only say they are likely to recommend someone to work there, they will actually do it.

→ **"Passives" score 7 or 8.** They are usually pretty engaged (7s and 8s are not low scores, after all), but the research shows they are less likely to do something about their positive sentiment, so they get the label of passive.

→ **"Detractors" score from 0 to 6.** These people won't recommend the organization, and if someone asks, they'll probably say something negative. From a research point of view, there's no point in distinguishing between a 1 and a 6—they all lean towards negative action, so they get the detractor label.

So, to get a single employee Net Promoter Score (eNPS), you take the percentage of your employees who are promoters, and then you subtract the percentage that are detractors. The NPS research indicates that when that single number moves up or down, it has an impact on the behavior (more so than, say, the overall average score going up or down).

That's all you need as a symptom metric. Let's say you've got 70% of your employees answering 9 or 10, another 10% answering 7 and 8, and the rest (20%) answering 0 to 6. Your eNPS would be +50 (70 minus 20), and that would be very high. We don't see many that get above that. On the other hand, we've seen organizations that had only 10% scoring 9 or 10, and a full 80% in the 0-6 range, so their eNPS was a -70. That's an indicator of a disengaged workplace.

A low score will tell you that you have a problem. Then you can use that information to do some deeper digging as to the cause.

The eNPS metric won't distract you by suggesting possible solutions, and that's a good thing.

Gather the Right Cause Metrics

To get to the cause(s) of low engagement (and, ultimately, the solutions), you'll need to dig deeply into workplace culture. Remember the basic equation from the last chapter (1.3 The Secret to Improving Engagement): Engagement is a result of a sharp alignment between individual success and organizational success, and the structures, processes, behaviors, and approaches that make up your workplace culture have a huge impact on that alignment.

To improve that alignment (and increase engagement), you'll need to make targeted shifts to your workplace culture.

Obviously, that means you need to understand your culture deeply, and that brings us to the topic of culture assessments. Like the engagement surveys, there are also a large number of culture assessments out there, and nearly all of them make one of two critical mistakes.

Culture Assessment Mistake #1

ASKING HOW EMPLOYEES FEEL ABOUT THE ORGANIZATION

I know that you want to know if your culture is "good" or not, but asking your employees how they feel about specific parts of your culture makes the same mistake that the engagement surveys make. You get data on what people like and don't like, but that is not the same thing as identifying the cause of a misalignment between individual and organizational success. People may report in the survey that they do not like the rigid divisions between departments inside your organization, but if those divisions actually protect the integrity and quality of the work, then it's not something you should change. Sometimes, unpopular policies are necessary for success. So, steer clear of culture assessments that present results in terms of percentage of "favorable" responses to each question, which are typically based on people simply liking different parts of the culture. They measure sentiment, but frequently miss the root causes of disengagement.

Culture Assessment Mistake #2

BENCHMARKING AGAINST ABSTRACT MODELS OF GOOD CULTURES

On the other side, you get culture assessments that are based on "best practice" research and benchmarks. They study many organizations in order to identify the specific characteristics that define "high-performance" cultures or a "best place to work." The Human Synergistics model, for example, suggests that you strive for higher scores in what they define as "constructive" styles (like being achievement-oriented or affiliative) and lower scores in what they define as "defensive" styles (like being confrontational or power-oriented). Their metrics tell you whether you have met those standards or if there is an imbalance.

The problem here is that your organization is unique, so whether or not you need to meet the "standard" is debatable, making the metrics less effective in providing guidance.

In the investigations of NASA following the space shuttle disasters,for example, culture was identified as a problem. It turned out that employees were not confrontational enough: It was taboo to challenge the expertise of the higher-up scientists, which meant that they were overlooking mistakes and inadvertently enabling tragedy. [4] Pointing to the model and encouraging NASA to be less confrontational would only make their specific problem worse. There is no one, universal standard for a good culture. You have to figure out what's right for you. Avoid the culture assessments that show you a "gap" between your score and the "good" score.

Culture Assessment Solution

MEASURE HOW PEOPLE EXPERIENCE YOUR CULTURE, AND PEG IT TO A "FUTURE OF WORK" SCALE

The secret to a good culture assessment is how well it captures how your employees experience the culture. A lot of assessments will measure "collaboration," for example, but with the specific angle of how well you enable collaboration, on a good/bad scale. Before you get to the good and the bad (since every organization's definitions of "good" and "bad" will be different), you need to know exactly how your culture approaches collaboration. If you ask people for help, do they help you? And does that only happen if you're in the same department? How rigid are the boundaries inside your organization? Can you work with people from other departments without needing permission?

Before you can evaluate whether you collaborate well, you have to know exactly how your culture does it in the first place.

For this, you will need to conduct a cultural assessment that will tell you exactly what your culture is and how people experience it.

The Right Scale: Traditionalist to Futurist

Instead of creating a good/bad scale, evaluate the elements of your culture on a scale of traditionalist to futurist.

DOWNLOAD: "FROM TRADITIONALIST TO FUTURIST"

This article contains more information about the future-of-work spectrum as measured by our culture assessment.

Remember the point we made in Chapter 1 about the Millennial generation and the big transition we're experiencing in leadership and management. Traditional management (think mid-twentieth century: command and control; only share information on a need-to-know basis; change is measured and controlled; consistency is valued over innovation) is becoming less prominent, and more organizations are adopting "futurist" principles like radical transparency, flexible hierarchies, enhanced inclusion and innovation, and a digital mindset.

The specific building blocks of your culture can all be measured along this continuum of traditionalist to futurist, instead of good and bad.

Let's go back to collaboration: If your culture is very territorial, and people rarely work outside their silo walls (or need permission to do so), then you'd be scoring more traditionalist in that area. On the other hand, if all your work is done on cross-functional teams, and you're constantly jumping between departments to get work done, and maybe you literally don't have walls or offices separating your departments, then you'd score more futurist. Each piece of your culture can be placed somewhere along this continuum.

You may be thinking, "Wait a minute! You said to avoid the good/bad measure, but obviously traditional is bad and futurist is good." Perhaps not.

At the big picture level, we would agree there is a general movement in management toward futurist. The pendulum is swinging in that direction, and at that big-picture level we think there is a lot that's potentially very good about that. Traditional management, for instance, was very engineering-oriented, and wasn't very good at meeting the needs of its employees as human beings. We think the shift towards being more human is a good thing.

But that doesn't mean every part of your workplace culture has to be futurist. If you are running a nuclear power plant, you probably shouldn't be too futurist around something like innovation. You don't want your people "hacking" internal processes or running experiments all the time—that would be dangerous.

The fact is, some parts of your culture will need to be more futurist than others... and that can change over time.

**DOWNLOAD:
CASE STUDIES**

Want more examples of how other organizations have explored these nuances within their cultures? Check out our case studies.

That's why your culture assessment must help you get very clear on exactly what your culture is. Understanding those details in terms of a traditionalist/ futurist scale is useful simply because management is in flux along those lines right now.

The better you understand where you are, the more effective you will be in figuring out which direction to go.

The Workplace Genome Model

In 2015, we joined forces with HR leader Charlie Judy to develop a culture assessment that we think does a better job of defining the "what is" of your culture, and it maps all the details along the traditionalist/futurist spectrum.[5]

Based on our research, we identified eight distinct Culture Markers to measure:

Workplace Genome® Model

CULTURE MARKER	DEFINITION
Agility	How the organization manages change.
Collaboration	How the organization facilitates working together.
Growth	How the organization develops its employees.
Inclusion	How the organization manages diversity and authenticity.
Innovation	How the organization is set up for the creation of new ideas and new values.
Solutions	How the organization incorporates internal (staff) and external (customer) user needs.

Technologies	How the organization leverages the digital age and utilizes current technology.
Transparency	How the organization communicates knowledge and builds trust.

Within each one of these Markers, there are eight associated Building Blocks meant to help you further understand your culture in ways that lead to effective action. For example, innovation is a hot topic these days, so a lot of organizations want to know if they are more traditionalist or futurist around that Culture Marker. We can give them a single score on Innovation, of course, but when they start to dig deeper, they realize that single score isn't enough. Here, for example, are the eight Building Blocks within Innovation:

Innovation Building Blocks

- **7.5** Future focus (N3)
- **7.2** Permission to hack (N7)
- **6.9** Inspiration (N4)
- **6.8** Creativity (N5)
- **6.6** Risk taking (N1)
- **6.2** Experimentation (N6)
- **6.1** Continuous improvement (N8)
- **5.9** Testing new ideas (N2)

A pattern we've noticed in our data so far is that a lot of organizations tend to score more futurist when it comes to the Building Blocks within the Innovation marker that focus on conceptual thought and ideation, like being future-focused and valuing creativity. But there are other building blocks that are more focused on taking action, like running experiments, taking risks, or beta testing, and these same organizations usually have more traditional scores there. These blocks allow you to identify patterns that give you a much better sense of how you actually "do" innovation in your culture.

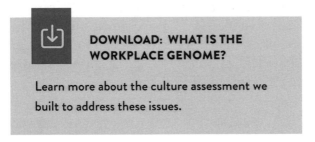

DOWNLOAD: WHAT IS THE WORKPLACE GENOME?

Learn more about the culture assessment we built to address these issues.

Let's bring this back to engagement metrics.

Spotting the patterns inside your culture is a critical first step to improving engagement.

→ **Step 1** - Understand your culture at a deep and nuanced level.

→ **Step 2** - Evaluate how that culture is supporting and not supporting the alignment of individual and organizational success.

→ **Step 3** - Design interventions to adjust culture so that organizational and individual success align.

You'll be lost trying to do Steps 2 and 3 without doing Step 1 first. That's why your culture assessment matters so much.

 # Don't Forget to Measure Your Change Efforts

Measuring root causes of disengagement is critical, obviously, but it's not the only thing you should measure. The whole point of measuring both symptoms and causes is so you can do something to address them. That means you'll be changing things, and as you change them, you'll want metrics in place to help you (a) know that you're making progress, and (b) change course if you need to.

Your change metrics are what's called "in-process" metrics. It's stuff you measure when you're in the middle of getting to the end result, and it's not a particularly strong suit for many organizations.

We tend to prefer the end-process metrics that tell us whether what we did worked. That's not enough when you are trying to improve engagement. Once you realize that a piece of your culture is interfering with individual and organizational success, you'll probably need to change several different things. As you're working on the changes, make sure you have some metrics that show you you're moving in the right direction.

You don't want to only gather your annual engagement at the end of the year to see if what you tried worked.

Let's go back to the innovation example above. Let's assume your culture is imbalanced on the concept/action ratio related to innovation (i.e., you're more "talk" than "walk" around innovation). Let's further assume that this lack of innovation is directly impeding both organizational and individual success. Your competitors are beating you to market with new products, and your people are frustrated that they can't make fast progress on their good ideas. As a result, you'd start to change processes internally to generate more actions related to innovation (experiments, prototypes, active hacking of existing processes, etc.). How will you know you're making progress? Here are some ideas:

Tip 1 ADD AN EXPERIMENT METRIC TO YOUR MONTHLY/QUARTERLY DASHBOARD

Literally track, by department, how many experiments were conducted during each time period and how many failed. (Side note: If all your experiments succeed you're doing them wrong; you're only experimenting on the things you know how to do.)

Tip 2 RUN A QUARTERLY PULSE SURVEY WITH STAFF

Ask about things they have done differently lately, or risks they have taken. Qualitative data is great as a progress metric too, and also helps to uncover new issues.

Tip 3 **USE TECHNOLOGY TO SUPPORT YOUR INNOVATION EFFORTS**

One example would be to implement an idea management platform like IdeaScale. That would help give you data on the very early side of innovation—how many ideas are being generated, and what percentage of the staff are participating in giving the ideas feedback. You could also track the ratio of ideas generated to experiments run.

These are just examples. You will have to come up with your own progress metrics after you start changing things. But don't forget to include these metrics in your overall plan.

2.6 Frequency of Measurement

We live in the internet era, which means we're all about data, and we think that's a good thing. With more data, we tend to make better decisions.

The downside of leveraging data is that you need to collect it in the first place, which usually means subjecting your people to lots of surveys.

And that delivers the issue of survey fatigue. If you google "survey fatigue," you'll get all sorts of advice about keeping surveys short, not asking for too much personal information, and making questions relevant. But we're not talking about random customer surveys. We're talking about the people who spend most of their waking hours with you. And on top of that, you're gathering data related to their experiences. In short, their tolerance for surveys is completely different. It's not about how long the survey is or what questions you ask. Whether they respond AND whether or not they provide good data is based on one factor more than any others:

Did you do anything with the data?

If you take no action on the data—or your actions seem clearly off the mark—then your employees will no longer trust the process.

And they will likely ignore future surveys or stop being thoughtful in their responses.

Or worse, they'll start to provide misleading feedback just to mess with you. They're not tired of taking surveys. They're tired of not seeing meaningful change.

Your surveys should be designed with a deeper understanding of what actions can be taken on the data you're collecting. Here's some tips for how that translates in terms of employee engagement.

Tip 1 **COLLECT SYMPTOM METRICS ON A QUARTERLY BASIS**

If you stick with the simple, one-question approach to measuring the symptoms (employee Net Promoter Score), then you can gather data more frequently. We see some organizations that are opting to measure this quarterly, particularly because you can slice and dice it to see how different departments, locations, or other subgroups are experiencing it. The eNPS is particularly good for tracking changes over time, so it lends itself to being measured more frequently. That way it serves as a leading indicator—changes in the eNPS let you know something needs your attention before it grows into a bigger problem.

Tip 2 **COLLECT CAUSE METRICS ANNUALLY OR BI-ANNUALLY ONLY**

You probably need to gather your base culture metrics once every year or two at most. The culture assessment you use should break the culture down into specific building blocks (see the Innovation Building Blocks, above), because then the patterns inside your culture will emerge and shine light on the factors affecting your engagement. When you see the patterns, it's much easier to get clear on your priorities and then develop action plans.

Tip 3 **COLLECT CHANGE METRICS AS NEEDED**

As we said above, these will be tied specifically to the change initiatives you've developed in response to areas of cultural misalignment, so it's a little harder to suggest a generalized schedule, but you'll probably want to measure this at least once a quarter so that you can make necessary adjustments as you are implementing your strategy. You might want to include periodic "pulse" surveys, through which you can gather small but specific packets of data from your employees. These can be as simple as asking your people, "Are we making progress on this priority?" Or if there are other quantitative measures of progress on your initiative, you could gather data on those. The data themselves are useful, but perhaps more importantly you'll derive some benefit by illustrating to your employees that you (a) heard their original responses, and (b) are already doing something about it.

The Dark Side of Benchmarks

Many of the culture and engagement metrics platforms out there will offer you benchmarking data. The "dummies" and "idiots" guides out there will tell you, emphatically, that it is great to compare your data to that from other organizations in your industry or vertical. We know this is tempting: The companies that we work with on engagement and culture definitely want to know how they compare. After all, this is subjective work. "Good" cultures and "deeply engaged" employees are hard to define, so it would help if we could know how we're doing compared to other organizations, they argue.

Here's the inconvenient truth: Benchmarks won't do you much good.

Knowing how you compare to other organizations that are similar will make you feel either good or bad, but it rarely helps you figure out what to do.

They tell you that you're different, but they can't tell you why—and it's the why that will guide your actions. Keep your eye on the ball here: You want analytics that will reveal how you are succeeding or failing at driving individual and organizational success. That, in turn, results in higher engagement. The bottom line, then, is that your analytics will be much more helpful when they focus on you, and your success drivers, and your specific culture elements—not the other guy's.

For example (back to our innovation example), let's say you've put some work into expanding the capacity for innovation inside your organization, because you can tie it directly to individual and organizational success. You then run your culture survey to shed light on how your employees experience the various components related to innovation (experimentation, beta testing, creativity, etc.).

And let's say on top of that you have access to benchmark data, so you can see how you rank— compared against those competitors you are trying to beat—on those very building blocks of culture related to innovation. Maybe you're more futurist when it comes to experimentation and beta testing, but more traditional around creativity.

So what?

If you are behind the industry when it comes to innovation, that is obviously relevant to what drives your success, but in our experience, the leaders who are behind are already well aware of that. And the details— which blocks you're ahead and which blocks you're behind—that level of comparative data is distracting. There are too many possible explanations for why those nuanced differences exist, and they are wrapped up in the internal workings of your competitors' organizations—workings you will never be able to see.

The benchmark data by themselves will never tell you whether or not you should emulate the competitors—or run in the exact opposite direction.

So, if you have access to benchmarking information, fine, but don't attach great importance to it. Double down on getting better culture assessment data in the first place, and you'll get much better results.

Since engagement is really the result of a culture that sharply aligns both individual and organizational success, you're going to have to up your game a bit when it comes to understanding what culture is and how to change it. We'll do that in the next chapter.

CHAPTER SUMMARY:
THREE THINGS TO REMEMBER

→ The source of engagement is the alignment of individual and organizational success—something that is missing from common engagement metrics.

→ Knowing what your culture is, specifically along a traditionalist to futurist continuum, is crucial to being able to improve it.

→ Take action, measure progress (not just results), and do something visible with the data you collect from employees.

CHAPTER 3

The Critical Link Between Engagement and Culture

By now it should be clear: Engagement and culture are joined at the hip. Engagement is a result of a crisp alignment between individual success and organizational success, and as we explained in the last chapter, the root causes of any misalignment are to be found in the building blocks of your culture. So, here's the basic process for improving engagement:

Engagement is a lagging indicator of culture. In other words, most of the work you will do to improve engagement is actually focused on your culture. So let's get serious about it.

 ## 3.1 The Four Core Elements of Culture

Culture can be a frustrating topic. Some definitions are overly simplistic (it's "the way we do things around here"), some are overly complex (it's how humans create meaning together), and without a good definition, the result is inaction, and that bugs us. So we tried to create a definition somewhere in the middle on the complexity scale that would help us move forward:

Culture is the collection of words, actions, thoughts, and "stuff" that clarifies and reinforces what is truly valued in an organization.

The first part of the definition (words, actions, thoughts, and "stuff") describes the elements where your culture comes to life through the people that work there.

Culture Element #1 **WORDS**

The terminology you use to describe your workplace.

The easiest way to think about this is to imagine a job interview, and the candidate asks you, "So what's the culture like there?" How do you answer? If you're like most people, you'll end up giving pretty superficial descriptions of culture (we have an awesome culture, it's fun to work here, we're like a family, here's our core values card...). That is only the beginning. What if you could be more detailed, clear, and specific when you describe your culture? If you could, it might sound something like this:

> *"Our culture is super focused on collaboration. In every project, we expect people to be working with people from other areas, and we literally tore down the walls and cubes to make sure people could have easy access to each other. If you're the kind of person who really likes to sit by themselves, headphones on, working solo, this may not be the place for you."*

That's just an example, of course. We're not suggesting that every culture should be radically collaborative like that. You could just as well present a description that talks about the importance of your silos and how protecting the work within each of your areas is critical to success. The point is that you are clear about what is valued in your culture and why. You go beyond platitudes and get to a level where people understand it deeply.

Culture Element #2 **ACTIONS**

The behaviors inside your workplace.

As they say, actions speak louder than words, so it's critical to ensure that your behaviors are consistent with the words you use to describe your culture. If the leaders tell you over and over again that this is a "culture of empowerment," yet your manager insists on sending your work up the chain for approval before sending it out, the behavior of the manager "wins." You will come to work knowing that you have a culture of getting approval (not of empowerment), despite what everyone told you.

Culture Element #3 **THOUGHTS**

The beliefs and worldviews your team members bring to the workplace.

This is more of a hidden layer of your culture—the underlying assumptions and mental models we have about humans and the workplace, which can sometimes lead to different perceptions and priorities in the workplace.

For example, sometimes some deep-seated assumptions that differ across the generations can actually play out in the culture.

In Appendix A on Generations we discuss the Baby Boomer generation and their emphasis on achieving work through teams, in-person. They may not realize it, but that could be a piece of the resistance some senior managers have towards supporting remote or teleworking employees. They may outwardly support the policy, but subtly end up undermining it because of their underlying assumptions about remote work.

Culture Element #4 **"STUFF"**

The physical and tangible elements of your workplace.

And finally there is the "stuff," or the tangible parts of your culture, like your office space design and decor, your dress code, your office location, whether people can work remotely, where people eat lunch, etc. We often take these things for granted, but these tangible elements also make it clear what's valued in your organization.

We know a CEO who was proud to tell us that the dress code in his organization was only two words: "No nudity." As long as you don't show up to work naked, you're fine. And people laugh at the policy, but there is a method to the madness. This CEO strongly believes that authenticity is critical to success in his organization. He thinks that he gets more productivity from people when they have the freedom to be their whole selves. So he intentionally chose a policy that encouraged that.

3.2 Why Values Matter Less Than Defining What Is Valued

The second part of our definition of culture gets at the ultimate purpose of your culture: to clarify and reinforce what's valued in your organization.

Notice that we used the word "valued" (with a "d"), as opposed to "values" (with an "s"). We did this intentionally to steer people away from the "core values" conversation. When we ask speaking audiences how many people have core values at their company, most hands go up. When we then ask them how many think those core values clearly drive the behavior inside the organization, nearly all of the hands go down.

You can have core values if you want, but if they don't impact behavior, then they are not relevant to culture.

After all, even Enron had core values like integrity and honesty hanging on the walls of their lobby—but that was clearly not what was "valued" in their culture. What was valued was making your numbers no matter what— even if you have to make a large accounting firm lie about it. So as you develop core values, do everything you can to make them specific and behavior-focused. The more tangible you make them, the more helpful (and relevant to culture) they will be.

 ## How Do You Tell a Good Culture from a Bad One?

Now that you know what culture is, let's talk about what makes them good versus bad. Not surprisingly, this is connected to employee engagement. Here's the short definition of a good culture:

A good culture is one where what is valued is aligned with what drives success.

Your culture makes it clear what is valued inside the organization. Once you are clear what is valued, that will drive your behavior. If those behaviors are sharply aligned with what makes both individuals and the organization successful, then your culture is good. And, as we're sure you have noticed by now, that alignment with individual and organizational success is what produces higher levels of engagement.

Here are two examples of how this plays out, one good and one bad.

Example: **GOOD CULTURE: A DELICATE BALANCE**

We worked with a small nonprofit organization that was providing some outsourced HR services to a large government agency, and that made their job sort of tricky. On the one hand, they were a small shop serving a small number of people in the agency, so that required hands-on, customized service to be successful. But they also reported to the higher-ups at the agency, which required the rigor, consistency, and often, red tape one might expect from a large bureaucracy. This pulled the nonprofit staff in different directions, which meant that one of their key success drivers was the ability to constantly maintain this "delicate balance" between inherently competing priorities.

When they started to clarify their culture, their highest priority became "we have each other's backs." In their culture, they had zero tolerance for sniping or complaining about people behind their backs. You always supported your colleagues. This sounds laudable, of course. Wouldn't every culture want that? Maybe, but the key part here is that not every culture truly needs it like they did. Having each other's backs was key to being successful in their unique environment. They were trying to balance the needs of the individual customers and the big bureaucracy, and could not afford to get distracted by office politics and rumor mongering. It threw people off, and made them less successful.

What made this good culture so effective was that they would not tolerate behavior that interfered with success.

A "bad" culture is one where behaviors that interfere with success are tolerated (and in some case rewarded). This includes the really horrible cases like those of Enron years ago or Wells Fargo more recently, but many bad cultures are less obvious and more difficult to spot.

Example: **BAD CULTURE: A ROVING PACK OF EXPERTS**

Once we worked with a technology company that had built its reputation on the quality of the subject-matter experts they deployed in each department or region. These people knew their stuff, and that set them apart from their competitors. But as they grew (particularly into new product lines), these experts needed to find ways to communicate their expertise to others in the organization. The company was scaling globally, but if people in one region were not aware of expertise in other parts of the organization, they would have to "reinvent the wheel" themselves, which was very inefficient.

Their culture, however, was not adapting to align with that need. The company maintained its traditional focus on hiring the smartest people, which was fine in and of itself, but it didn't support or develop the kind of access or connectivity among all those smart people that would enable both individual and organizational success. As a result, their people were operating more like "roving packs of experts," than a unified organization.

> Different departments who needed to collaborate on sales, for instance, were generally unable to get the right information at the right time. Things started falling through the cracks. Deals were being lost. Visible mistakes became more commonplace during implementation. This led to lower engagement and increased turnover.

This "roving packs of experts" aspect of their culture was a problem specifically because it was interfering with the success of the enterprise.

Why Does Culture Change Seem So Hard?

At this point, people tend to connect the dots and start to get a little nervous, because they realize that in order to improve engagement, they are probably going to need to change their workplace culture. That's scares people. People tell us all the time that culture change is hard, if not impossible, and that it will require years and years of effort, extensive change management, copies of *Who Moved My Cheese,* etc.

This simply isn't true.

We have seen a culture radically transformed in less than 12 months. One organization went from a low-performing, fear-based culture (the only time Management ever physically entered the cubicles was when they were firing someone), to a high-performing culture based on transparency and employee focus, all in 12 months. It was hard work, and they had to make tough choices (including firing a number of senior people), but culture change can happen quickly.

So how do you do it? At one level, your challenge is absurdly simple and obvious and involves three steps:

1. **Get clear about what your culture is;**

2. **Identify the parts that need to change; and**

3. **Start doing things differently to achieve that change.**

It sounds straightforward enough, but in reality, it must not be, since relatively few organizations do it successfully. They say they're going to do it, but they don't. They start to do it, but they don't finish. They try to do it, but they fail.

Why? Because each of the three allegedly simple challenges above (what is your culture, how should it change, what will you do to change it) contains a hidden challenge that nearly everyone misses.

Hidden Challenge #1 **BEING HONEST ABOUT WHAT YOUR CULTURE IS**

When people start doing the work of defining the current culture, they end up off track because they don't know how to describe their culture in a deeply honest way, capturing it just as their people experience it, complete with contradictions, faults, idiosyncrasies, and everything else. It seems too hard, so

CULTURE 101

A brief course about how to define your culture and understand culture change.

we either stay at a fairly high level (the core values path), or we dive right into defining the ideal culture, focusing only on the parts of our culture that we like.

If you don't start with a completely honest picture of "what is," then your people may miss the direction you want to head in—or worse, they won't trust it.

When you tell me we need to move in a new direction, but that seems disconnected from my current experience of the culture, I will question your direction. But when you describe our culture in intricate detail, and that description matches my experience, I'm now much more open to discussing with you where we go from here.

It is easier to get behind culture change when the story makes sense.

Story: **GETTING INNOVATION OUT OF THE SILOS**

One of the organizations we worked with was exhibiting the pattern we mentioned in the last Chapter, where cultural building blocks related to the conceptual side of innovation (e.g., creativity, future focus) were far more advanced than those on the action side (e.g., experimentation, beta testing). The data also revealed an interesting contradiction. The specific building block related to "hacking" things was actually quite developed in their culture, compared to lower scores in the other action-oriented building blocks. If people are hacking existing processes, why aren't they running beta tests or experiments?

Their answer was an important realization for them: You can hack something by yourself. If you want to change something you're working on, that's easy to do alone. But if you want to run an experiment or plan a beta test, it is more likely to overlap with what others are doing. Innovation was only occurring in silos or individual work streams, but they hadn't developed a culture where it was done collaboratively. Once they identified and named that dynamic, it seemed almost obvious—yet they had never addressed it before.

With a clear picture of the deeper reality of their culture, it then became much easier to map a path for changing it.

For you to overcome this hidden challenge, you'll want to start with a culture assessment that gives you really good data (see 2.2 Gather the Right Cause Metrics), but on top of that, try to stay disciplined in your ongoing analysis by employing practices like the "five whys" technique to try and get to the hidden truth inside your culture.[6] Once you come to a conclusion (e.g., we're not innovative enough), ask why? We emphasize innovation concepts over taking action. Why? We don't want to interfere with the work of other departments. Keep up your inquiry until you get to parts of the culture that have not been previously articulated, yet are consistent with people's experience and tie back to what makes them more successful.

Hidden Challenge #2 **CONNECTING CULTURE PRIORITIES WITH SUCCESS DRIVERS**

After you articulate what your culture really is, you must determine how that culture is affecting individual and organizational success drivers so you can figure out exactly what needs to change. Again, this seems like a fairly straightforward challenge—if you can see your culture for what it truly is, then you should be able to identify the trouble spots that need fixing. But in reality, there will always be more trouble spots than you can handle. Remember, culture is all the words, actions, thoughts, and stuff that clarify and reinforce what's valued in your organization. That covers a lot, so there's almost no end to the number of specific things you could try to improve.

And when you have that much choice, you frequently feel paralyzed or end up spreading out your change efforts in too many directions, which results in little progress.

Instead, you need to be rigorous about improving the specific parts of your culture that will have the biggest impact on what makes both your employees and your organization successful.

What's really interesting is that many organizations struggle to identify their specific organizational success drivers. They can give you generic success drivers— more sales, better productivity, focus on the mission— but they can't get more specific, and often have trouble identifying the factors that make a difference in their immediate work. You need to get more specific in order to identify priorities for your culture change.

For example, asking what you are admired for (both internally and externally), and what parts of your culture you think needs to be preserved at all costs and yield useful insights as a starting point.

Coming up with clear answers to questions like that will help you identify the success drivers that are most important, right now. One company we worked with had recently completed a number of acquisitions, and they were very clear that revenue growth was important for positioning the company for a possible future sale (that was one of the obvious drivers). But as they dug into both their culture data and some of the above questions, they realized that a critical avenue for that growth facing them right then was to become a "one stop shop" for their customers, incorporating the products and services from some companies they recently acquired into their offerings.

This allowed them to focus their culture change efforts. They made it a priority to build more common ground and unity across the various parts of the now larger company, and they started developing action plans that would facilitate moving in that direction. (Note: we'll get into details about what those action steps look like in the next chapter.)

Hidden Challenge #3 **MAKING CHANGE EFFORTS SUSTAINABLE**

And that—action plans that move your culture in a new direction—brings us to the third hidden challenge. There is something about culture change that makes it very difficult to sustain. Unlike many other change initiatives, culture has a strong tendency to revert back to the way it was when we're not looking. Why? Because culture is autonomous.

Culture, unlike many other parts of your organization, has the power to move, change, grow, and evolve without you lifting a finger. In fact, that is culture's default mode: evolving and growing organically.

Does that sound familiar? You keep deferring culture until you "have time" to deal with it. You're dedicating more of your attention to issues related to strategy or implementation of existing processes. You definitely have a culture, but you can't really say what it is. If that's you, then you have what we call a culture "by default." Even if you ignore it, the culture is living and growing on its own.

The alternative—a culture "by design"—is usually more effective, but you will always face the challenge of making your designed culture sustainable, because there is a strong gravitational pull back to the default mode, where your culture evolves on its own. The same is not true for other important parts of management. If you were to drop the ball on financial management, for example, the organization would quickly fall into disarray, and you'd have to respond. But because culture can chug along just fine by itself, it is hard to make intentional culture change sustainable.

There is hope, however. Each of the next five chapters is focused on helping you make your culture change sustainable.

3.5 Introducing The Playbook Model

In the next chapter, we present a model for culture change (and improving engagement) based on creating and implementing a straightforward "playbook." Sorry for the sports metaphor, but we have found this to be the best model for designing long-term, sustainable culture change and growth. It always requires a number of different plays that you run at different times. After the model, we give you three chapters that dig into three specific major types of plays (process, design/structure, and technology), and we'll close with practical advice for embedding this kind of work into your organizational structure and processes.

CHAPTER SUMMARY:
THREE THINGS TO REMEMBER

→ Culture is the collection of words, actions, thoughts, and "stuff" that clarifies and reinforces what is truly valued in an organization.

→ A good culture is one where what is valued is aligned with what drives success.

→ There are three hidden challenges to understanding your culture: being really honest about what it is; connecting it to success drivers; and making changes that are visible, sustainable, and lasting.

CHAPTER 4

The Playbook Model for Improving Engagement

The business world loves ideas. Come to think of it, maybe that's why so much of our professional lives are dedicated to "the meeting." We get people together, we discuss things, and we generate important insights.

And then too often nothing happens.

Here's an employee engagement example of that dynamic. A large enterprise conducts an extensive annual engagement survey and distributes division-specific results, expecting action from the leaders. In one division, the scores around the category of agility were particularly "unfavorable." An internal team was then convened, and after several meetings they developed a slide deck (of course) that included the following message:

Don't just say you're agile—BE agile!

This is the epitome of our focus on ideas over action. All this team had was the insight that the people in the division needed to embrace agility, but they had no concrete idea how to do that (other than enthusiastically telling them to do it).

What does "be agile" mean? How do you do it? What will you change? What behaviors will be different? We have to start answering these questions in organizations, and we need to do it quickly and easily if we want to see better results.

Turning back to our sports analogy, if you're the coach and your team is losing the game, you don't turn to your players and say, "Score a goal!" (the equivalent of "BE agile!"). You give them a specific play to run—a series of coordinated actions designed to achieve a specific objective. The same is true with culture and engagement.

If you really do think that agility is going to help your people and your organization to be more successful, then develop some plays that you can run that will support more internal agility. Some plays will be high risk, and others will be low risk. Some shoot for really big results, and some might be incremental. And most importantly, some are just not going to work, so we need to have some other plays in your playbook to run when a play breaks down.

For every important insight related to either culture or engagement, you should be ready with a number of "plays" that you can run inside your organization that will move the needle.

Without knowing what to do next, your insight is useless.

How to Use "Plays" to Shift Your Culture

In the context of culture and engagement, a "play" is an intervention designed to make your culture more tightly aligned with what makes employees and the organization more successful, which will increase engagement. In short:

A "play" is something that you either create or change about the way you do things in your organization to move your culture in the direction of the culture priorities you have identified.

As a quick reminder, we discussed how to set "priorities" in the previous chapter (Hidden Challenge #2: Connecting Culture Priorities with Success Drivers). Your culture priorities are (perhaps obviously) the areas that have the biggest impact on success. So the plays that you develop to improve culture and engagement should be targeted directly at those priorities. This helps you avoid focusing only on the urgent, short-term, surface-level problems, a common mistake in engagement work.

DOWNLOAD:
PLAY TEMPLATE

We've included a template for a culture play, that you can use to identify things you can do to change your culture.

In the previous chapter, we shared the example of a company that was growing through acquisitions and realized they needed to become a one-stop-shop for their customers in order to grow. Their culture priority was built around seeking "common ground and unity." To do that, they developed plays, and like any organization, they had three options.

Option #1 **CREATE SOMETHING NEW**

To shift culture, you'll often want to introduce new things to change people's behaviors. One of the plays that the company seeking common ground and unity developed was to create a brand new position in the company: the "brand ambassador." This role would be created in each product line to be the go-to person for questions about how to connect with other products.

Option #2 **CHANGE SOMETHING THAT EXISTS ALREADY**

A lot of your internal processes will still be good enough to keep, you just need to make key changes to them to make sure they contribute better to everyone's success.

As an example, one of the more extensive plays the company mentioned above wrote up was to make sweeping changes to the company intranet that were focused specifically on enabling people in different parts of the organization to see how others could connect to the work they were doing more quickly and clearly.

Option #3 **STOP DOING THINGS**

This one, frankly, doesn't get enough attention, but there is actually research that shows you can make more progress by removing obstacles that are in your way, rather than trying to develop new programs to go in a particular direction. With this in mind, one of our other clients actually proposed a play that created a new committee whose specific job was to analyze and make recommendations for stopping existing programs.

 # **Where to Focus Your Plays**

Plays, of course, could address just about anything inside your organization, but if your focus is on culture and engagement, you'll want to zero in on a few specific areas where the plays are likely to have a bigger impact.

→ **Rituals and Artifacts.** Culture runs deep, so parts of it will be symbolic. Make sure you are intentionally crafting and shaping those symbols to align them with your success drivers. This includes things like a "culture code" slide deck, or annual celebrations.

→ **Stewardship.** Culture needs to be protected and nurtured over time, which means you need processes or structures inside your organization to do that ongoing work. This could include cross-functional culture teams or annual processes where culture is evaluated and changed.

→ **Talent/HR.** This is perhaps an obvious one when it comes to culture and engagement, but the way you hire, the way you do performance management, the way you recruit—these are all critical to shaping culture and improving engagement.

→ **Process.** This is the broadest of the six categories, but let's face it—most of your work day is spent engaged in one kind of process or another, so this is a big area for culture. Staff meetings, organizational metrics, quality control, budgeting, strategic planning. There are many processes that you could change to start moving the needle. We'll go into detail about process plays in Chapter 5.

→ **Structure/Design.** This one may feel abstract, but structure and design are critical, and cover two distinct areas. The first is organizational design— your org chart, roles and responsibilities, job descriptions, lines of authority—that has a big impact on culture. But the other is more tangible—office space design, which is equally important. We'll go into detail about design plays in Chapter 6.

→ **Technology.** These days we had to give technology its own section. The way you employ technology tools, from things as basic as having a shared drive for storing files, to specific software applications like idea management software, collaboration tools, or intranets—this all impacts culture and engagement. We'll go into detail about technology plays in Chapter 7.

 ## 4.3 Brainstorming Your Plays

Okay, presuming that you overcome the second "hidden challenge" and you have come up with a short list of clear priorities for your culture that will make you more successful and improve engagement, then your next job will be to brainstorm a list of plays.

Keep it simple to start. Develop a separate list of draft plays for each priority that answer two basic questions:

1. **What will you do?**

2. **How will it move the needle on the priority?**

Let's go back to agility as an example. If agility is truly a priority, then your initial plays might revolve around giving more authority to certain levels of the hierarchy, because it would allow them to take action instead of waiting for approval. Or maybe you'd implement technology to make more information visible throughout the system, so people wouldn't have to wait for email responses about tracking down the information. As you develop each play, note that it will have a specific "what" and a "why."

The plays will probably be all over the map in terms of their level of effort, the time commitments involved, and the impact they have on the priority, and that is fine.

In the end, you'll want to have a mix of plays in your playbook, some of which are "quick wins" to show your team that you're actually doing something about this, and others might be really "big ideas" that could take a year or longer to put in place—but have a large impact on the priority.

As we mentioned back in Chapter 2, you might even want to develop some metrics specifically around each priority and what moving the needle will look like.

Once you have your initial list brainstormed, you'll want to go back to it and add in some of these details around level of effort and impact. And if you can, it would help to flesh out your approach to the play and identify possible action steps that will be required during implementation. You don't want to plan the whole thing out—that happens later. But you'll want enough detail identified so you can take the next step, which is prioritizing your plays.

Prioritizing Plays

Depending on how many culture/engagement priorities you're working on, you could end up with a long list of plays—we've seen companies quickly develop 40 or 50 to add to their Playbook. Obviously you can't run 50 plays at once, so it is important to prioritize your list.

One quick way to start thinking about the priorities is to distribute your plays on a 3x3 matrix based on level of impact on the priority (vertical axis; low, medium, high) and level of effort required (horizontal axis; low, medium, high).

If you find some plays that are low effort and high impact (upper left)—they would most certainly be among the first you implement. But you'll more likely see that your plays skew from the middle to the upper right—medium and/or high in effort and impact. (And, for the record, if you have written down plays that are high effort and low impact, you'll get a "see me" note from the teacher.)

DOWNLOAD: EFFORT/IMPACT MATRIX TEMPLATE

Download an example of this matrix that you can use as a template for your plays.

It's important to note here that the effort/impact matrix is just a first step in prioritization. It won't only be about identifying the highest impact plays. Remember that what you are doing here is culture change. As we mentioned earlier, sustaining culture change will require a mix of both short-term, visible victories, along with longer-term infrastructure changes.

Here's a simple framework for sorting out your plays. Identify one of the following three categories for each play:

→ **Big idea** - high investment but high return, technically complex and/or costly, many departments involved, applies broadly across the enterprise or touches a lot of areas, resources (staff time) needed, etc.

→ **Meaningful improvement** - manageable degree of difficulty, strong payout, meaningful impact; requires multi-department collaboration; important problem solved or new opportunity opened up for internal or external stakeholders; reaches a sizable number of people.

→ **Quick win** - low degree of difficulty, inexpensive implementation, targeted impact; focused number of departments; fast to market idea that's worth doing.

You'll want to narrow down your plays to a small number to start with (we'd suggest no more than ten, but it could be fewer than that). In your initial list, you'll want a few quick wins, no more than one or two big ideas (to start, anyway), and the rest meaningful improvements. The point here is that you want to send a clear message to your people that you're committed to two things:

Commitment #1 **MAKING IT REAL**

The quick wins are designed to show people that you are serious about moving the culture in the direction of the priority. It's not just the management flavor of the day—you actually are changing things.

Commitment #2 **MAKING IT PERMANENT**

The meaningful improvements and big ideas are there to show people that you're in it for the long haul—this is not just window dressing.

If you don't accomplish both, you'll start to see resistance.

 ## Defining "the Ask"

As you create a prioritized list of plays, you will need to add a new section to your Play document: "Ask from Management."

Since improving culture and engagement require either doing new things or doing things differently, someone needs to approve them. This won't happen unless someone in the organization provides the money, or time, or space for them to happen.

So for each play, you should develop a specific "ask" of Management. This could be a budget request, or approval from supervisors for a cross-functional team to be created. In some cases, a play that was developed by people in one department might require collaboration from people elsewhere in the organization, so someone higher up in the chain needs to create the space for that to happen, either by releasing people from other obligations or maybe even adding headcount.

The level of detail in the ask will vary depending on the nature of the play. For the big ideas, it is likely that some kind of higher-level task force will need to be created simply to spec out the details of the implementation. For quick wins, you might be able to make a request with a fairly complete task list along with it. But either way, these plays require an organizational commitment, so someone needs to be asked for that.

4.6 Playbook or Backlog?

Once you have your playbook created and have some kind of management approval to get started, you may find that the "playbook" metaphor starts to break down a little. As much as we love metaphors, we're okay with that. Technically, a playbook features plays that aren't modified very often, and they represent a menu of actions you would try in any given circumstance. Your culture and engagement work doesn't quite work like that.

Plays are designed to be implemented and then evaluated as to whether they have successfully moved your culture in the right direction, but once they are done, move on.

As you complete plays in your playbook, you need to start adding new ones designed to continuously make more progress on culture and engagement.

Once you're into implementation you may want to switch to a metaphor related to agile software development:the backlog.[7] In agile software development, a cross-functional software team will develop a backlog of specific aspects of the software that need to be developed, and on a regular basis (often weekly), they will prioritize which parts of the backlog need to be worked on, and those get pulled out and addressed that week. At the end of the week, some will be complete, therefore taken off the backlog entirely, and others may have been delayed or refined, so they go back into the backlog. The new list is then re-prioritized for the next week, and the team starts work on the new list.

Your culture work is similar. As you run plays, the quick wins will be complete and come off the backlog, or perhaps they aren't working so you will need to tweak them and try them again. The meaningful improvements and big ideas will need to be broken down into smaller tasks that get implemented and managed over time. And down the road, you'll probably identify new plays to add to the list. In the end, the work of culture and engagement is continuous.

Now it's time to get specific about the plays. We pulled out three of the major types of plays (see 4.2) to highlight in this book: Process, Design/Structure, and Technology. We'll start with process, because this is likely where the lion's share of your culture/engagement plays will be.

CHAPTER SUMMARY:
THREE THINGS TO REMEMBER

→ A culture "play" is something that you either create or change about the way you do things in your organization.

→ Changing culture involves brainstorming lots of plays: big and small, short term and long term, different levels of effort.

→ All plays should move the needle on a culture priority you've identified—otherwise you're still addressing symptoms, not causes.

CHAPTER 5

How to Create Processes That Don't Suck

Your workplace is essentially one big collection of processes that your employees implement every day. We go to meetings, we share information, we do budgeting, we do expense reports, we do performance reviews—we use processes to implement these things. You probably even have a process for planning the company picnic.

The good news is, that means your processes can provide a lot of leverage for shifting your culture and improving engagement. We encourage you to design a number of plays for your playbook where you make tweaks to your processes, change them wholesale, or even eliminate existing processes and create new ones.

If you can do that in a way that helps your people be more successful, then you will improve engagement.

Yet this isn't just about making processes better in general. You can spend a lot of time "optimizing" your processes without improving engagement. Changing the agenda of your staff meetings because you think it will help them end in 45 minutes rather than an hour is fine, but until you can make the case that that specific change will help your people be more successful in ways they couldn't access before, then it's not a play for your culture and engagement playbook. That's the standard here.

Take a hard look at your processes. Nothing should be off the table, no matter how long you've been doing it that way, and even no matter how successful it appears to be.

Even processes that aren't objectionable might need to be modified to support the behavior that will drive success and engagement.

Obviously there will be some processes that are very unique to your organization, but below we give some areas you might want to explore.

 ## How to Transform Your Meetings

This is a huge one. The work day for many of us consists mostly of meetings, and generally speaking, we don't like them. But our complaints are all over the board—they are too long, they are too short, we need to stay on task, we never talk about the important stuff, we have too many people in the meetings, we didn't get the right people in the meetings, and so on.

If you want better meetings, then start designing them based on the actual outcomes you hope they will achieve. Form follows function.

We got this lesson from Patrick Lencioni's awesomely titled book, *Death by Meeting*. Are there people in your organization who say they refuse to come to a meeting unless an agenda of topics is presented ahead of time? Well, Lencioni presents a model for a weekly tactical staff meeting where the topics are not generated until the meeting begins. For example, if your goal is to identify and address whatever "fires" have emerged over a seven-day period, start the meeting by listing all the fires—something you could not possibly do the week before (when they weren't actually fires yet). Once you have all the fires out on the table, you decide as a group which ones you want to tackle in the next 45 minutes and then you do some action planning. That's it.

And if someone tries to bring up a bigger, strategic topic, politely refuse. That's not the purpose of this meeting, so we're not going to talk about it. Those issues are covered in monthly "strategic meetings." Those meetings do have an agenda sent ahead of time, often with additional data sets or homework to help people prepare for the meeting. They last two hours instead of one, and most of the discussion time is focused on clarifying and understanding the strategic issues and their drivers, rather than tactical action planning. The point is, when you have a different kind of outcome, you design a different type of meeting.

Here's a secret pro tip: Shaking up the way you do meetings can even help you make some subtle shifts in the way you manage your hierarchy.

We know one organization that not only embraced the monthly "strategic meeting" concept, they also chose to revolve who would be in charge of leading the meeting, which includes fleshing out the topic, identifying the homework, and pulling together the data. It turned out to be a great professional development opportunity for some of their entry level employees, who had never been given that kind of responsibility. Here are some examples of meeting-related plays.

→ **All Hands Meetings.** These are periodic meetings where the entire organization gets together at the same time to hear presentations from the CEO or top leadership. We're seeing a lot of organizations suggest this as a process play in their Culture and Engagement Playbooks, and it addresses priorities related to transparency. People need to hear what the very top of the organization is thinking, doing, and focusing on. If you don't tell them, they'll make it up (and usually something worse than the truth). In traditional meeting structures, information cascades down (senior team tells the directors, the directors tell their reports...etc.), but having a single meeting where everyone hears the same thing can be very powerful. Some smaller organizations have adapted this idea into a slightly different version: a daily stand-up huddle with all staff simply to share what everyone's working on. The visibility helps people see important issues or conflicts before they emerge.

→ **Cross-Functional Connections.** These usually start as informal get-togethers, just to give people an opportunity to learn more about what people in other departments do. From there it can expand to regular, more targeted meetings that solve problems based on input from multiple areas. This play addresses priorities related to collaboration, and it's a good example of a "quick win." It doesn't have a huge impact, and it's easy to implement, but it makes it clear in the culture that you need to be valuing cross-functional collaboration.

How to Transform Your HR Processes

Technically, Talent/HR is its own section of the Playbook, since all of your HR and talent work has a clear impact on culture, therefore engagement. But since we're talking about processes, we would be remiss if we did not mention some of the key HR processes, since they are frequently included in playbooks.

If there's any part of an organization that is known to be "process-oriented," it's Human Resources. They have detailed processes scripted for hiring, performance management, onboarding, tracking vacation days, enrolling in health insurance...you name it. In fact, this is arguably one of the biggest problems in HR—they are too focused on process and administration, leaving them very little time and attention to give to the deeper and, frankly, more important things like culture and engagement (which we also put on their plate). We are forcing them to have a split personality, and it's almost impossible for them to pull off.

So the approach here should be to connect the two halves of the work.

How can you weave culture and engagement into the administrative processes? Are there processes you could either reduce in scope or eliminate that would help your employees be more successful?

The more your HR processes are aligned with culture and contribute to individual and organizational success, the better they will be. Here are some examples of talent/HR plays.

➜ **Hiring.** Menlo Innovations, a software company we wrote about in *When Millennials Take Over*, created a hiring process that is specifically focused on their cultural priorities around collaboration. Since their software coders use the "pair program-ming" method, collaboration is essential (if you share a mouse with someone, you'd better know how to collaborate). So the first round of their hiring process is a group interview where candidates are paired up and given an assignment to complete together—and they are told that they'll be evaluated on how well they help their pair partner (their competitor!) get through to the next round. For this software company, it is important to focus not only on technical ability, but also the culture of collaboration that enables and facilitates that technical work.

EXCERPT, *WHEN MILLENNIALS TAKE OVER* (2015)

Read more about Menlo Innovations in this excerpt.

→ **Performance Reviews.** An Australian association changed its performance management process to be better aligned with culture and engagement in a couple of significant ways. First, they changed their numerical ratings to more specifically address the 12 pillars of their culture that they had spent time articulating in the previous year. They did not ask questions like, "Is this employee performing above expectations?" Instead, they asked, "Is this employee behaving in ways that are consistent with each of our cultural principles?" Interestingly, when they made that switch, one of their senior managers decided to leave after the clarity of the new process helped him to see that he did not feel comfortable working within the new culture. The organization responded positively to this, and actually helped him find a new job. Second, they asked employees to talk about how their work there was helping to fulfill what they believed were their destinies. Yes, destiny.

Engagement is tied to your employees being personally successful, and success will look different to each based on their priorities and goals.

You don't have to use the word "destiny" if you don't want to, but in this day and age (particularly with Millennial employees), if you're not in touch with employees' ambitions, hopes, and motivations, then you might end up struggling with engagement.

DOWNLOAD: MAKING PERFORMANCE MANAGEMENT WORK

Read this white paper for a deeper dive on this thorny topic.

How to Transform Your Metrics

Here's a disturbing trend: The amount of data we collect inside our organizations is increasing, yet at the same time, our bandwidth for measuring and analyzing that data is rapidly declining. That means the pressure is on.

We'd better be careful about the things we choose to measure and what we do with the results.

As a process, however, organizational metrics are stuck woefully in the "we have always done it that way" mode. We have a fairly standard set of financial metrics that we track periodically, and each of the major departments or deliverables inside the organization has their set of data that we track on an annual basis at least: units sold, number of registrations, number of hits on the website, employee turnover rate, etc.

There's nothing wrong with all those metrics, but isn't it odd that they haven't changed much in the last 20 years? We can state with some confidence that these organizations are facing significantly different realities today, as compared to previous decades. That means their success drivers have changed, which means their internal behaviors need to change, but as long as they measure the same old data, their attention will go in the same old places. That's a problem.

If you need to shift your culture, then change what you measure and when you measure it.

Find out what kinds of data will spark meaningful insights and start collecting and analyzing. This may require some experimentation, as the data sets may not seem intuitively to be what you need, but you won't know until you try. Here are some examples of metrics-related plays.

→ **Experimentation Metrics.** This one comes up in the context of innovation. You won't get innovation if you're not running any experiments and testing new ideas in the real world. But too many organizations simply declare the need for innovation, without having the discipline to put metrics in place to make sure those experiments are actually happening. So here's a simple fix: Add experimentation metrics to your organization's monthly or quarterly dashboard. Have every manager report up from their department how many experiments they ran, along with what percentage failed. (Note: the failure part is key, because that's where most of the learning comes from.)

→ **In-Process Metrics.** It is extremely helpful to measure progress while you are working, rather than only after your efforts have concluded. Take employee engagement: We've seen many organizations conducting frequent "pulse" surveys to track engagement. Some of our clients track their employee Net Promoter Scores (see Chapter 2) on a quarterly basis (rather than annual) so they can identify trouble spots and patterns before it's too late. We are also working with clients to develop in-process metrics related to the specific culture priorities that they developed as guidelines for their plays. Some, for example, have developed priorities related to transparency and increasing internal communication, which typically involves many different individual plays, some of which take a fairly long time to develop and implement. As they are working through them, they could add some questions to the quarterly pulse survey to get some qualitative assessments from staff on whether or not transparency and information flow were improving.

How to Transform Your Information Sharing

In addition to measuring data and generating insight from it, you also need to share it internally (though the how and why should vary per your organization's cultural priorities). But it is not always easy to ensure that the right people have the right information at the right time.

From a culture point of view, our information sharing processes show up consistently around the "silo" issue. We have tons of data, but they tend to be locked behind departmental lines, which means that valuable information is not shared, and the organization rarely takes all of it into account as a whole. The answer to this problem, as we discussed above, cannot be simply to have more meetings, so we are challenged with creating processes that will create a smarter data flow, without taxing the system in terms of time and effort to share the information.

The main cultural issue here is transparency, though we don't think everyone needs to be completely transparent all the time. It should be more strategic than that.

To make your people successful, the goal here should be to make more things visible to more of the right people in order to improve the quality of the decisions that get made throughout the organization.

Take a hard look at your system and find out where more information would help people make better decisions and start there. Here are some examples of plays related to information sharing.

→ **Meeting Agendas, Materials, and Notes.** This is a very simple play to run—make the information that's shared inside meetings available to everyone, or at least more than the people who were at the meeting. We see organizations doing this particu- larly for meetings among senior managers. When more is visible, employees are more likely to make decisions that are in line with the overall strategy and direction. And if you want to be radical about it, just follow online publishing platform Medium's lead: If more than two people have a meeting in that organization, notes must be created and placed on the shared drive. Everyone in the organization knows what is discussed at every meeting.

→ **Intranets.** Creating (or improving) an internal intranet or other collaboration software is an example of a heavier play, but one that can produce big results. Technology allows for asynchronous communication that can be easily searched and sorted, which allows people from all over the organization to access just the information they need, when they need it. Too often, companies deploy technologies like this with only a generic goal of amassing "more information," but the more successful plays will connect the specific features of the technology with the immediate culture and engagement challenges.

We'll discuss these more in the Technology chapter, and there are some interesting developments in this area related to artificial intelligence as well.

How to Transform Your Decision Making

We don't often think of decision making as a "process." Decisions seem more like an action. People just make decisions—in every department, every day. That's how work gets done, right? Not exactly.

We have processes for making decisions, even if some of them are somewhat informal. There are certain people that have to be involved in decisions, or at least sign off on them, before they can be implemented. We often set standard procedures for deciding how much data and analysis are needed before a decision can be made.

Focusing on how you make decisions might sound sort of boring, but it's a huge opportunity for improving engagement.

Around the water cooler you'll hear people lamenting the bad decisions that were made, but what many don't realize is that if we had developed a smarter decision-making process, the bad decisions could have been avoided in the first place.

Are you mad that your competitor was able to beat you into a market before your team could pull the trigger on developing that new project? Maybe if you hadn't had so many people attending every meeting, you could have worked faster. Annoyed that the new technology rollout failed...again? Maybe your decision-making process failed to reveal the competing priorities among two key departments. As the examples below illustrate, getting rigorous about decision making can directly impact performance.

→ **The RACI Model.** We had a client that specifically needed to increase the speed of their decision making. They highly valued "inclusion" in their culture, but realized that it resulted in too many cooks in the kitchen when it came to making decisions, and that was slowing them down. So one of their culture plays was to implement the RACI model into their project management processes. For each project, they assigned internal roles: Responsible (the person doing or deciding), Accountable (the boss above that person), Consulted (person you must consult with before deciding or acting, though you're not obligated to take their advice), or Informed (the person who hears about the decision after the fact). It took a little time to set this up in the beginning, but it sped up their decision making significantly because it gave everyone a clear (and more limited) role in the decision-making process. Instead of lots of meetings with lots of people, there were focused meetings and more targeted communications directed to the relevant roles. The process still included everyone, but it was much faster.

**CASE STUDY:
IMPROVING SPEED AND AGILITY**

Read more about this particular example online.

→ **Criteria Transparency.** We know of some organizations who have developed rigorous processes for making their decision-making more transparent. When evaluating the appropriateness of an enterprise software package, for example, each of the senior members would start by ranking the importance of the criteria for making the decisions (see 7.5 Innovation for the specific example of decision-making software that can help with this). Through illuminating key differences, they were able to refine their list of criteria, making the ultimate decision-making process simpler and more effective.

Processes get a lot of attention in culture and engagement work, as they should—they are all about how things get done so they are great for modifying behaviors that will make people more successful. Our next chapter tackles a section of your culture and engagement playbook that doesn't usually get as much attention: structure and design.

**CHAPTER SUMMARY:
THREE THINGS TO REMEMBER**

→ Improving processes for the express purpose of helping employees be more successful will result in improved engagement.

→ Think about plays involving processes where people get together: meetings, information sharing, decision making.

→ Another obvious place to come up with plays is around talent, performance, and measuring data.

CHAPTER 6

How to Improve Engagement Through Design

Leaders frequently undervalue the impact of design and structure on their organizations, but they shouldn't.

When you created your organization chart, you probably put some thought into who reports to whom, but did you even consider whether or not a standard hierarchical structure was right for what you're trying to accomplish? Did you consider that the concept of middle management might be a thing of the past?

We rarely design our organizational structure with intention, beyond filling in names inside a structure that has been standard for more than a century. And the same is true when it comes to the more tangible design of our office space.

There are some interesting debates raging these days about the new "open office" designs, but whether you put everyone at a shared table, give them individual offices, or send them all into Dilbert-style cubes, the ugly truth remains: The decision was probably made after a couple of senior people met with the architects to map it out, likely with efficiency and cost-saving in mind—not culture or engagement.

If we really want to improve engagement, we need to start thinking like designers. Your culture and engagement playbook might include some serious re-designs of both organizational structure, and physical workspaces. But don't think about it like a kitchen remodel—replacing that laminate countertop with granite and upgrading with cool new appliances and cabinets. That's not what we are talking about. We are referring to truly marrying form and function and using design to reflect the values and processes that will make your people and organization more successful. You'd be amazed at what a well-designed space can do for an employee's capacity to be successful.

 ## Resolving the Open Office Debate

We have to start by ending the pointless debate about the "open office." For every article out there extolling the benefits of doing away with "cube farms" in favor of communal tables, there's another showing how damaging such designs are to productivity, since everyone is constantly distracted and spreading each other's germs.

Here's the truth: Every single, possible workspace design works well—except when it doesn't. I know that's frustrating, but it's true. Humans need to work together, and they need solitude. They need bustling, energetic environments, and they need calm, quiet ones. They need introversion and extroversion.

Don't ask whether you need an "open" office plan. Instead, ask what design will make your people more successful.

If the job of your department is to record podcasts, then of course your people need individual offices—maybe even with soundproofing. But if your department is responsible for analyzing and documenting emerging market trends, you might want everyone within earshot of each other so they can connect the dots between what they are working on and what others are working on.

In the research for *When Millennials Take Over,* we came across two successful software companies. One (Menlo Innovations, one of our case studies we mentioned earlier) uses an open office design. Everyone works together in one big room on tables with wheels that can be moved around as needed. The reason for this is that they use a process called pair programming, where two coders share one computer and write the code collaboratively, and this was tied directly to what makes them successful. They found the process generated consistently higher quality code, which meant fewer bugs to fix later and very satisfied customers.

They also rotate people through the different projects to keep them fresh, so putting everyone in the same room means that they can quickly have conversations with others who may have worked on a particular project with minimal disruption to their work flows. The way they design their workspace is tied directly to what makes everyone there successful.

EXCERPT, *WHEN MILLENNIALS TAKE OVER* (2015)

Read more about Menlo Innovations in this excerpt.

The other software company does not use pair programming. They have found success through a combination of solo work and collaborative work, with a strong focus on supporting each employee's uniqueness and unique approach to software design. On the office space side, they let employees choose their workspace—some work at communal tables, but one works best in a private office that is lit only by Christmas lights.

In both of these examples, the office design was intentional and based on how the structure of the workspace would help people succeed.

So instead of picking a side in the debate, start to be intentional about your workspace design. Get clear on what kinds of collaborative spaces and solitude spaces you'll need to be the most successful. It will probably be a mix, but the ratio will vary based on your context, not what you read in the business press.

 ## It's Not About Preferences

Coming up with the right structure/design plays for your engagement playbook is definitely going to require that you talk to your people. This is true of any good design process—you talk to your customer to ensure that the form and the function are aligned.

But with office design, we don't always do that. Sometimes senior management assumes that the employees will make unrealistic demands if asked for their input on office layout and design, so they don't ask at all. And when we do have the courage to gather data from staff, we tend to focus our inquiry on their individual preferences. Would you prefer your own office to a cube? Would you prefer open office design versus private offices? Would you prefer departments housed together or spread out?

That's a mistake.

While it is good to involve your employees in the design of your office, don't ask them what they would *like*. Ask them what would make them more successful.

Story: **DESIGN AROUND THE NEEDS OF YOUR EMPLOYEES**

Take the example of a nonprofit in Arizona that was engaged in a complete cultural transformation. They didn't ask staff for general suggestions about an ideal workspace. They specifically asked them what changes to design would make them more successful. When improving success was the primary criteria, the answers became more specific and applicable to the goal of driving engagement.

Among other things, this non-profit runs a suicide prevention hotline, which is a very stressful job, to say the least, and during breaks, they don't have a lot of time (or a space) to relieve that stress. They suggested installing an exercise room near the call center, which management agreed to immediately—not to address a "preference," but to help them better serve people in need.

Another department had a very different request, however. This was not a high-stress department—they did long-term policy work with state agencies and mental health services. Every new policy challenge required a wide array of expertise, all of which could be found internally. But the people with the right expertise were hard to identify. The employees suggested that an open workspace could help them be in better contact with their teammates and, consequently, know who has the knowledge to tackle specific challenges. In response, management created a "puzzle room" for them to encourage informal interaction and exchange.

In other circumstances, an internal gym and a puzzle room might seem like unreasonable demands, but since they were targeted specifically at what would improve the performance of those involved, they had a direct effect on engagement.

 ## Millennials and Office Space

Don't bother Googling to find out if Millennials prefer the open office design versus traditional offices—you'll get both answers. When you look at the big picture of what shaped the Millennial generation, there are some important lessons to bear in mind as you plan out your office space. (See Appendix A for more background on generational differences in the workplace.)

Lesson 1 **FOCUS ON FLEXIBILITY AND CUSTOMIZATION**

Part of the digital transformation we've experienced over the past few decades has been a shift in the balance of power—away from the makers of things, and toward the users of things. Think about it—software no longer comes with user manuals, because if the software doesn't work immediately (in a way that makes sense to the user), then the users will quickly move on to a different product. Millennials grew up in this world and have come to expect that focus on the user, and the ability to customize their experience. That means that one of our office design challenges moving forward will be to create spaces that allow for flexibility and customization. How can you create a space that will allow for different people to work in different ways? How would you have to modify your space to allow for people to work at different times, or in different configurations?

One nonprofit we worked with redesigned their space to be radically focused on the "user" (i.e., the employee). Employees can opt for a standing or seated desk. They can choose between collaborative, coffee-shop-style work spaces, or take a break in the super-quiet yoga room. They even have wi-fi on the roof. Even small changes like this will drive engagement. As one employee put it, "This places cares more about us, so we should care more about this place."

Lesson 2 **FOCUS ON MULTI-LAYERED (ONLINE AND FACE-TO-FACE) COLLABORATION**

Growing up with Internet and social networks, Millennials are used to constantly networking and connecting to others. They get instant feedback through apps like Instagram, and in school they were given more opportunities to do group projects than generations past. Even college libraries now have floors dedicated to collaborative (and noisy!) work. As University of Tennessee researchers point out, Millennials "have been working in teams their whole lives."[8] Yet traditional office design creates some natural barriers to collaboration. Collaborative work has to be scheduled in an office or conference room, rather than emerging as needed. As we said above, this doesn't mean you have to swap out all your cubes entirely for giant work tables, but if you have an opportunity to move into a new space or redesign your existing one, you might want to consider expanding the percentage of physical space that reduces the barriers to collaboration.

Lesson 3 **FOCUS ON WHERE YOU CAN PROVIDE ACCESS TO HIGHER LEVELS**

One of the most common complaints about the Millennial generation is that they were given too many trophies as children. This is part of a broader narrative about Millennials being coddled and spoiled, therefore they can't take negative feedback and see themselves as more special than they are. We disagree. Research suggests that Millennials did receive more focus as children (particularly compared to Generation X, who were known for operating on their own), but this focus was part of an overall elevation of the status of children in society. Millennials' parents engaged with them differently, effectively giving them more access to and influence on the adults with the power, compared to children of previous generations. Millennials expect that kind of access and voice in the workplace. This can include easier access to more senior people, but also across silo lines.

We knew of one organization that was so siloed, the different departments were on different floors, and your key card only gave you access to the floor that your department was on. Millennials will not understand restrictions like that. They expect to be able to access others in the organization regardless of their hierarchy, and even if they are not connected to that person on the org chart.

THE OVERLOOKED CONNECTION BETWEEN COLLEGIATE DESIGN AND WORKPLACE CULTURE

A fascinating study about how disconnected workplaces are from how recent graduates entering the workforce are used to collaborating and learning.

 6.4   # Resolving the "Silo" Debate

Speaking of silos, let's talk about the other half of the design equation—organizational design. Just like office design, organizations are often stuck in the "we've always done it that way" mentality when it comes to organizational charts and reporting relationships. The CEO is followed by a line of VPs, who are followed by vertical departments, and each one headed by a director. Those vertical departments, carefully aligned and separated, generated the "silo" metaphor. The walls aren't literal (except in the key card example above), but sometimes they might as well be. People in different departments often struggle to share information across those "walls" or do things collaboratively.

So we hear lots of calls to "bust" the silos. From an org chart perspective, this was the birth of "matrix" management, where people started reporting to lots of other people (hmmm, how could that end badly?). The open, collaborative work spaces were often designed with a silo-busting mentality as well. Yet departments still exist, and looking at the culture data we've been collecting over the last few years, silos persist. So are they good or bad?

The answer isn't so simple.

The fact is, sometimes we need silos. Sometimes your finance people need to work by themselves, relying on finance and accounting expertise that the others do not possess—in fact, involving others would likely lead to more errors. And at the same time, we need the boundaries between our silos to be permeable.

If department leaders have no access to financial information or are unable to work with the financial experts as they are doing their planning, then department budgets could end up being way off, and we might even have difficulty making payroll.

So just like office space, you're going to need to design some plays that make your organizational structure more effective, without relying on the oversimplification of "silos versus matrix."

 ## How to Reinvent Your Organizational Structure

As mentioned above, some organizations, like Zappos, are running experiments with making fundamental changes to organizational structure, like embracing Holacracy.

HOLACRACY: THE NEW MANAGEMENT SYSTEM FOR A RAPIDLY CHANGING WORLD

We highly recommend this book by Brian J. Robertson (Henry Holt and Company, 2015), which explains a complex yet fascinating way of reorganizing management structures.

Holacracy is an "operating system" for an organization that replaces the traditional organizational chart with a series of "circles" that can form and dissolve as specific organizational issues need to be resolved. Others, like W.L. Gore & Associates (makers of Gore-tex), have long been known for their different approaches to structure. From a hierarchy point of view, Gore & Associates breaks their whole organization down into just two titles: leader and associate (and the associates have the power to give and take away the title of "leader"). They also won't let divisions grow larger than about 150 people before they break them into more divisions (based on anthropological research that revealed that community groups lose the sense of intimacy when they grow beyond 150 people).[9]

Both of these examples imply fairly radical and wholescale structure change, but that's not your only option. Here are some examples of things you could do that don't require a complete transformation.

Tip 1 TURN YOUR ORG CHART INTO A COMMUNITY

In this day and age, why on earth is your organizational chart only in a word doc? Why isn't it live on the internet, where it can be annotated (and updated) with detailed information about what people do, what specific expertise they have, and what projects they are working on? While you're at it, maybe you can add some functionality for comments and conversations. Or document sharing. Just because you're divided into departments, doesn't mean there can't be visibility across silo lines.

Tip 2 **BUILD OUT A SYSTEM OF SHADOWING AND JOB ROTATION**

The traditional approach to gathering people from different silos is to create cross-functional teams. There's nothing inherently wrong with getting people from different departments together to work on projects, but too often they end up being more of a burden and a distraction since everyone on the team would rather be focused on their primary job. But sending one or two people to go work with another department for an extended period of time is different. They get the benefit of the cross-functional collaboration and information sharing, without the pressure of having to do two jobs at once.

By the way, if you conclude that you can't spare anyone to go work in another area for an extended period of time, then you might be choosing short-term efficiency over longer-term success and growth. In other words, collaboration and learning about other departments takes time—which is inefficient in the short-term, as you're taken away from your immediate tasks—but the whole point of learning about the other groups is that you will be able to apply the knowledge later in a context you haven't envisioned yet. It's an investment that pays long-term returns.

Tip 3 **CREATE INTERNAL CENTERS OF EXCELLENCE**

Some of the companies we work with are building out ways in which experts from different departments can share their knowledge with the rest of the organization (through activities like lunch and learns) or actively provide services to internal "customers." The purpose of asking people to spend a portion of their time on internal-facing work (as opposed to functional or billable work for external customers) is to help a larger number of people in the organization get access to that information and to be more successful through access to the distributed expertise. Management often pushes back against these efforts, citing how "expensive" it is for these people to be taken away from their "real" jobs. One of our clients wanted to calculate the opportunity costs of establishing a Center of Excellence. The members of the leadership development group acknowledged the cost, but then compared it with the arguably greater cost associated with people wasting time searching for the information they needed in the organization.

CHAPTER SUMMARY:
THREE THINGS TO REMEMBER

→ If we really want to improve engagement, we need to start thinking like designers.

→ Design your workspace to address what people need to be successful—NOT their "preferences."

→ Don't make the mistake of oversimplifying a desire for open vs. closed spaces or siloed vs. matrixed design according to what seems "cool" in the business press. All organizations need some of each.

CHAPTER 7

How to Improve Engagement with Technology

In today's technology landscape (particularly HR technology), it is easy to become overwhelmed by "shiny object syndrome." Every technology solution out there claims to be the one thing you need, the one thing that will move the needle, the one thing that will create powerful cross-functional synergy, best-in-class performance, an engine for innovation and growth, and through-the-roof employee engagement (how's that for brochure copy!).

The problem is that every new technology seems to create as many new problems as it solves.

What we need today may not be what we need tomorrow. Even the software creators recognize that they may need to transform their product several times in order to keep up with the marketplace.

We need to stop pretending that there is a shiny object "answer" out there, and let's start taking a more practical approach to our technology use when it comes to culture and employee engagement.

Here are some tips:

Tip 1 **EXPECT TO USE MULTIPLE TECHNOLOGIES**

This can be a challenge, because some people really like the idea of integrating everything and are on the lookout for the one product that can do ALL the things you need. To be fair, it is a lot of work (and work-arounds) to integrate 19 different software products, but since the goal is to make everyone in the organization successful, it's possible that integrated, multi-functional products may not work for every employee's needs. Get ready to go small. The good news is that software designers are getting better at modular integrations, so it is now possible to have multiple software components working effectively together without requiring them to be combined in a single package.

Tip 2 ASK WHETHER THIS TECHNOLOGY WILL GENERATE MEASURABLE CULTURAL RESULTS

When you are at the point of writing plays for your playbook, you need to be very practical. The whole point of a play is to make internal adjustments to address priorities related to shaping culture, and ultimately increasing organizational and individual success. For example, we see lots of organizations developing culture priorities related to transparency—they want to make things more visible so their people have the information they need to make smart decisions. So if you are evaluating a new tool like Slack, visibility and better decision making should be your primary evaluation criterion. When evaluating technology tools, hone in on the "why:" Why would using this tool move the needle in the right direction?

Tip 3 EXPLAIN THE "WHY" BEHIND THE TECHNOLOGY

This is critical, in fact, to ensuring broad adoption of a new tool. In Chapter 3 (Hidden Challenge #1: Being Honest About What Your Culture Is), we pointed out that if you can't paint an honest and convincing picture of your current culture, your people may not trust the new direction that you are proposing. It's the same with the "why" of software. When presenting, it is okay to highlight the non-engagement related features it will offer, but start by making it crystal clear to everyone how this new product will drive both individual and organizational success. This will significantly reduce resistance.

And then start experimenting. Here, we present some of the technologies available for driving engagement. You'll need to do your own research to find out what kind impact they might have on your specific cultural goals. In today's ever-changing software environment, a few of these tools may have been transformed or acquired by the time you read this, but you can see an up-to-date list of culture-related tools and services at culturetools.net.

CULTURE TOOLS:

For an up-to-date listing of tools related to improving culture (and engagement) go to culturetools. net. This video explains how the site works.

7.1 Intranets and Communities

Intranets and online community products are frequent features of client playbooks these days, particularly when organizations are larger than 150 employees. Larger enterprises are looking for solutions that can scale engagement.

Powerful intranets can often check more than one box for you— interactive org chart, space for conversations, even functionality related to some of the categories below, like feedback and performance management.

These plays tend to fall into the "high-investment, high-return" category. Some examples:

→ **Jostle (jostle.me).** Dubbed a "people engagement" platform, it covers events, newsfeed, and "shout outs" to fellow employees. Jostle includes an organization chart and employee directory (with expertise info) and facilitates team discussions to encourage collaboration.

→ **Sitrion (sitrion.com).** Key features include ideas and surveys, expert search, document sharing, and tools for employee communications. They tout it as the one employee app you'll need, and they integrate with enterprise-level products from Microsoft, Oracle, SAP, etc.

→ **Igloo (igloosoftware.com).** Igloo calls their product a "digital workplace solution," focusing on communication, collaboration, knowledge management, and culture. Its features include blogs (and microblogs), file sharing, forums, people directories, collaborative virtual spaces, and to-do lists.

Collaboration and Project Management

This is one of the more "evolved" categories, as some of the software solutions here, like Basecamp, for example, have been around for quite a while (in software terms, anyway). One of the primary benefits of all of these products is reducing and redirecting email traffic into other forms of communication so that information, documents, and momentum are not lost.

While on the surface these products are fairly logistical in nature (tasks, calendars, gantt charts, etc.), they are typically deployed as engagement plays to break down silo walls and improve agility.

→ **Asana (asana.com).** Focused on organizations (they make it hard for you sign up with your Gmail address), this software product allows you to create projects and tasks that are assigned to individuals on the team. At the more advanced levels, you can create and share dashboards and also accomplish basic communication and information sharing related to the various projects.

→ **Basecamp (basecamphq.com).** Basecamp is also organized around organizing teams, projects, and tasks, but puts more emphasis on document sharing.

→ **Zoho (zoho.com).** This one is designed specifically to work for software design teams, though its functionality certainly works for other teams as well. The product includes a "traditional" project management option as well as an option that enables managing "sprints" (a process in agile software design). You'll find classic project management features here like gantt charts and tools for tracking billable hours.

→ **Trello (trello.com).** This platform is more focused on straightforward team collaboration than full-service project management. You create "boards" on which you can place "cards" that have details, to-dos, and even threaded conversations.

→ **Slack (slack.com).** This tool is far on the collaboration side of the spectrum, allowing teams to communicate and share information more effectively. Teams can create "channels" where they can post messages, making them easily visible without having to read things that are not relevant to what you are working on.

7.3 Feedback and Performance Management

In the Process chapter (5.2 How to Transform Your HR Processes) we mentioned that performance reviews are a frequent target for changes related to culture and engagement—if engagement is about being successful, then it follows that we should be measuring success somehow, and performance reviews can at least partially fill that need. There are many, many traditional performance review software programs out there (for filling out annual forms, etc.), and for larger enterprises, these types of software are often built into the bigger HRIS platforms (ADP, BambooHR, Zenefits, Namely, etc.).

Visit the online resources for a list of some tools that are specifically focused on performance management (or giving and receiving feedback) that support frequent, even real-time feedback.

These solutions tend to be treated as engagement plays for professional development or encouraging an employee-focused culture.

→ **Small Improvements (small-improvements.com).** Declaring that the annual review is "dead," this solution focuses on supporting 1-1 meetings, real-time recognition, 360-degree feedback, and an interesting review process where ratings consist of a "dot" placed on an open 2-axis scale (and you define the axes).

→ **iRevü (irevu.me).** This tool can be integrated into a larger, annual performance review process, and focuses on requesting, giving, and receiving specific feedback. It allows people to provide feedback in the moment (or shortly thereafter), rather than making feedback a scheduled chore that is part of the annual performance review process. The tool allows you to connect each piece of feedback to the unique cultural priorities or values in your organization, as well.

→ **PropFuel (propfuel.com).** As the name indicates, this platform started as a recognition software (see the next section for those) but has since evolved. It still allows employees to give each other positive reinforcement ("props"), but the main features are now focused on enabling both employees and customers to provide feedback to the company. The software allows you to create pulse surveys with specific, targeted questions, and then track the results of the feedback over time to generate insights.

Recognition and Rewards

If you take the concept of feedback and marry it with some kind of spot compensation to the employee (financial or otherwise), then you have entered the realm of recognition software.

Where feedback tools tend to focus on professional development and performance management, recognition tools are more about motivation and morale.

There is some danger here, because financial rewards tend to focus people's attention,so it's critical that the rewards are geared specifically for factors that will strengthen culture and overall organizational success.[10]

Some studies have shown, for example, that individual financial incentives for performance actually led to a decrease in team communication.

→ **Bonusly (bonus.ly).** A classic example of the points/rewards version of recognition. Employees give each other recognition through the platform, which earns them points that can be cashed in for rewards.

→ **Teamphoria (teamphoria.com).** Also a classic example, but rewards/recognition is just one component of this engagement software (they also have pulse surveys, performance review, and communication).

→ **Motivosity (motivosity.com).** Motivosity replaces points and rewards with cash. The system gives each employee a set amount of actual cash to distribute to peers as spot awards. Money they receive can either be spent on company-defined merchandise or gift cards.

→ **Globoforce (globoforce.com).** This is reward/recognition software focused on the large enterprise. Users have access to advisors who help you figure out exactly how many points to assign to different kinds of recognition, and they even have a system for "microcasting" recognition stories, sending them to targeted, smaller groups inside a larger enterprise (because if you try to "share the success stories" with everyone, it can be a flood of information that ends up being distracting).

7.5 Innovation

In the context of engagement and culture, innovation refers more broadly to the capacity to do things differently, run experiments, and be creative.

With this in mind, the most relevant category of tools is "idea management," but we're also giving some examples that focus on mind-mapping and decision making.

→ **IdeaScale (ideascale.com).** This tool is billed as an "ideation community," and it has specific applications for different markets, including technology, government, nonprofit, and small business. The software is straight idea management, from ideation, to refinement, to merging, reviewing, and implementing.

→ **Spigit (spigit.com).** More appropriate for large enterprises, it has more sophisticated functionality for managing ideas that come from a larger universe of individuals, offering separate treatment for ideas coming from employees, partners, and customers, for example. The tool also includes AI-powered analytics.

→ **Sketchboard (sketchboard.io).** An "online endless whiteboard," this is a visual approach to idea management and feedback, allowing team members to share and develop ideas collaboratively online. It integrates with other communication platforms, rather than trying to include them in its own interface.

→ **Transparent Choice (transparentchoice.com).** This software offers a suite of products related to project management, but at the heart of it all is a structured process for prioritization and making decisions in a more transparent way. Everyone who participates spends time ranking the criteria they use to evaluate decisions, and the software then helps them structure some conversations where they resolve any differences, so the end result is clearer criteria for prioritizing. We view this as a piece of innovation, as it offers the opportunity to clarify what you will put resources into and why.

7.6 Wildcards

One of the cool things about the software space these days is that you simply can't keep up with it. There are always new tools, new solutions—sometimes to problems you didn't even know you had. Or, more likely, problems for which you figured there couldn't be an online solution. Well, there probably is. Visit the online resources linked below for some miscellaneous tools that support your efforts related to engagement and culture.

→ **Jane.ai (jane.ai).** This is a digital assistant powered by artificial intelligence. It scours all of your apps, systems, documents, and websites for information and then allows employees to ask questions and get custom answers via a simple chat interface. This tool is particularly relevant when facing challenges related to silos and transparency.

→ **Wevue (wevue.com).** This tool enables communication within an organization, primarily via photos and videos (and emphasizing the use of your smart phone). The goal is to use it to strengthen culture through interaction, as short phone-recorded videos and video montages allow employees to share their personal lives and connect with coworkers. It also includes pulse survey capability.

There will always be new tools. This is just a taster.

The key here is to think about not just what the tools can do functionally, but how you can implement them as plays in your culture playbook.

As anyone who has implemented new technologies in their workplace probably knows, the technology is often the easy part. What's much harder is getting buy-in from everyone, which is why the "why" is so important. And that leads us to the next question: Whose job is engagement?

**CHAPTER SUMMARY:
THREE THINGS TO REMEMBER**

→ Think about technology differently—not just software tools' stated purpose, but how they might move the needle on culture and engagement.

→ Intranets, communities, and project management tools can directly address better internal collaboration and information sharing, but only with everyone's buy-in.

→ Culture and engagement software is hot right now. Look for HR tools for performance management, continuous feedback, and innovation/idea management for some creative solutions. But always be clear on the "why" and what culture priority you're trying to improve.

CHAPTER 8

Whose Job Is Engagement?

We have introduced many new possible culture process changes in this book, so at one level, it would appear that everyone in the organization is going to be involved in improving engagement in one way or another. At the same time, however, we cannot let ourselves fall into the trap of declaring that engagement is "everyone's job." That line is overused (culture is everyone's job, quality is everyone's job, inclusion is everyone's job...), and it's not getting us anywhere. You know why: If everything is important, then nothing is important.

Improving engagement is not "everyone's job." If you make something everyone's job, eventually you will find that no one is doing it.

Alternatively, we could just put this on the plate of "leadership." Take the highest levels of the hierarchy and let them know that they will now be held accountable for higher engagement (and a stronger culture). Unfortunately, that sometimes yields the same results (i.e., nothing). Often the highest levels of leadership are overburdened, with very little bandwidth to manage the efforts that truly affect engagement, but they are also often somewhat removed from the front lines of the organization, and that's where the everyday work—and engagement – happens.

So who does that leave us with? Conventional wisdom says Human Resources. That's where most organizations put the responsibility for employee engagement by default, and it's not without logic.

We do believe HR has a critical role to play in improving engagement, but it cannot only fall on their shoulders.

By now you should see the conundrum here: Engagement can't be everyone's job, yet it doesn't seem to belong to any single individual or group either. To solve this puzzle, we need to go back to our definition of engagement.

8.1   ## Clarifying the "Job" of Engagement

Definition of engagement from Chapter 1:

> *Employee engagement is the level of emotional commitment and connection employees have to an organization that is driven by how successful they can be at work, both personally and organizationally.*

Process for improving engagement identified in Chapter 3:

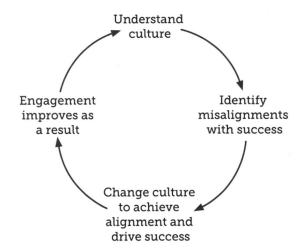

The "job" of improving engagement, therefore, integrates culture change and the alignment of individual and organizational success, and that is a really big job. In fact, we put that job at the same level as some of the more established core organizational functions, like financial management. Finance typically has its own department with headcount, but on top of that it has created systems and processes that extend into other parts of the organization (budgeting, reporting, expense reimbursement) to ensure the finance function is working smoothly. It's a system-wide job, in the end.

For some reason, we don't give culture the same level of attention, even though the job is equally complex and challenging. To turn that around, we need to embrace what we are calling "culture management."

Culture management is a system of activities, processes, and technologies that an organization uses to understand, shape, and change its workplace culture on an ongoing basis.

It's not complicated. When your culture management system is strong (i.e., it does a good job of aligning culture with individual and organizational success), then it will improve employee engagement.

So instead of assigning employee engagement as someone's job, let's commit to creating a strong culture management system. And for that, we think HR needs to step up and lead the effort.

It's Time for HR to Step Up and Lead This

We presume that a significant portion of the readers of this book come from the field of Human Resources. That's good! We want HR to read this book, because we believe HR should take the lead on creating and sustaining strong systems of culture management. You won't have to do it alone, but if you don't lead it, culture management will likely end up on the back burner, and engagement will stay right where it is.

But we need to have a blunt conversation first. HR, as it currently stands, is not set up to succeed in leading the culture management efforts. This is not due to lack of talent or intelligence—there is no shortage of smart people in HR. This is about the entire field of Human Resources being rooted, deeply, in a traditional and engineering-based approach to running organizations, and that happens to be fundamentally out of sync with the requirements of culture management today.

This goes back to what we said in Chapter 1 about the Millennials (1.4 Aren't the Millennials Changing Everything?). Leadership and management are changing to be more human. That, in fact, is one reason why culture has become more important and visible lately. Human beings (and particularly Millennial humans) care about culture. Human Resources, however, has been built on a foundation of process, compliance, risk avoidance, rules, efficiency, and scalability, which is fine in some contexts, but those concepts are all rooted in an engineering mindset. Think about it: You actually call the human beings in your organization either "resources" or "capital." And you're okay with that. This is an engineering mindset, and it presents us with a big problem:

You can't use an engineering mindset to generate engagement among human beings.

Culture management requires a strategic, systemic, and more human view of the organization, one that can successfully align what makes your individual humans successful with what drives the success of the whole enterprise. We didn't use to ask HR to manage things like that, but now is the time for you to step up. We need you to design and lead a strong system of culture management. Let go of your compliance mindset. Let go of wanting to "own" the process in a controlling way. Stop asking for your "seat at the table," and just take it. Roll up your sleeves; this will not be business as usual.

Here are a few tips for where you might want to start.

Tip 1 START BY EMBEDDING CULTURE ROLES INTO YOUR ORGANIZATIONAL STRUCTURE

Where does the work of culture management happen? You probably don't currently have people in positions that are exactly aligned with the work of culture management, and the sooner you fix that, the more visible culture management will be. Don't let that hold you back, of course—get people working on culture management even if you can't change their title right away. But words and structure matter, so if culture and engagement are nowhere in the org chart, it might be harder to get the work done.

Tip 2 MASTER THE METRICS AND MEASURE PROGRESS ON CULTURE

Culture analytics is typically measuring the right things (specifically, 2.1 The Ultimate Question for Employee Engagement and 2.2 Gather the Right Cause Metrics). You may want to phase out your annual engagement survey and replace it with some sharper metrics that get at the cause rather than the symptoms (culture assessments, dynamic pulse surveys, etc.). And then once you've actually developed some culture priorities and start running some plays from your playbook, you may need to develop a whole new set of metrics that focus specifically on how you track progress against the priorities (e.g., how would you actually measure improved cross-department collaboration?). Over the long term, you'll want to connect those to improved engagement metrics (employee NPS) and other core performance metrics.

Tip 3 **RUN SOME STEWARDSHIP PLAYS**

We talk more about culture stewardship below (8.6 The Holy Grail of Stewardship), but setting up who will mostly be organizing the culture work should probably be a top priority for you, in order to establish your role as the leader of the Culture Management System. Take the lead in creating a cross-functional "culture team," for example, to serve as an informal (yet powerful) group for articulating and advocating for the culture work (see more below).

It's time for HR to take on culture management. Of course, if you're not in HR, there are a few things for you to pay attention to as well.

What CEOs Need to Know About Engagement

A friend of ours once said,

> *"As a CEO, I can't drive the culture single-handedly... but I can kill it in a heartbeat."*

As the CEO, you have to be involved in culture management. Truthfully, you don't have a choice, because even if you ignore culture altogether, everyone is watching your behavior, and they will use that to draw conclusions about what is valued at the organization, whether you want them to or not. So you'd might as well be intentional about it. The good news is that you have some flexibility for how you can become involved in your organization's culture management efforts. Here is some advice for finding your engagement-based leadership approach:

Tip 1 **MAKE THE SUCCESS DRIVERS YOUR PRIORITY**

Even if you are delegating the primary work of culture management to others in your organization, make sure you have a strong presence when it comes to the work of identifying strategic success drivers. As CEO, you probably know more than just about anyone about strategic success factors, so this is a particularly important role for you. Employees have a tendency to move in the direction that they think the people in charge want to go. If you don't make your culture goals, objectives, and priorities extremely clear to everyone (and connect them with the success drivers), they will fill in the gaps with their own assumptions and inventions. Don't let that happen. For example, if a culture team is developing a set of culture priorities, make sure you schedule meetings with them to share your insights about success drivers so they become integrated into what they are doing. This is much more effective than responding to them after they've been developed.

Tip 2 **BE VISIBLY INVOLVED IN SOME OF THE PLAYS**

When you start to move the culture in the direction of the culture priorities, everyone will need to know that you're behind them. It helps to have to least one play that features you prominently (example: leading a virtual "town hall" meeting). This is what we call a "making it real" play in 4.4 Prioritizing Plays. Your actions matter. Your people want to see you living the culture.

Tip 3 **BE CAREFUL OF WHAT YOU TOLERATE**

Once you make a commitment to move the culture in a particular direction, you have to back it up. So if one of your senior managers isn't living that commitment, you can't give them a pass. You'll hear different versions of this quote, and they are all right: "Culture is defined by the worst behaviors leaders will tolerate." (Or, one bad apple...) If you are committed to doubling down on collaboration in order to be more successful, but one of your senior managers is annoyed by all the new meetings she needs to go to, claiming it's taking her away from

CULTURE MANAGEMENT FOR CEOs:

This online course provides additional insights and advice for CEOs.

the revenue generation you're expecting of her, for instance, you cannot let it slide. If collaboration is what matters, you have to hold her accountable to that. This is why making your cultural priorities (and associated behaviors) visible and clear to everyone is so important —so there's no doubt about what's expected.

What Managers Need to Know About Engagement

Those who have other people reporting to them inevitably play an important role in culture management. Here are some of our favorite tips and advice for managers:

Tip 1 **BE A CONNECTOR**

Outside of the CEO, technically all managers are "middle" managers in the sense that they both report to someone and have people reporting to them. One of the burdens of management is that you're always torn in two different directions, trying to make everyone happy.

When it comes to culture and engagement, individual happiness is not the goal. Individual success is.

One of the best ways to speed up success is to get out of the way. Instead of occupying the middle trying to please everyone, start to connect the people above you and below you directly. Let's say you're working on a play in your playbook around information sharing internally. Try to let people below you work directly with people above you on defining a new process for information sharing (instead of trying to "manage" it yourself). Not only might they start solving more of their own problems, but each party will also learn something about the other, and that will strengthen your culture management work generally as well.

Tip 2 **GIVE THE GIFT OF TIME**

We have noticed that many organizations—small and large—complain about a lack of time, and use this as an excuse for not working on culture like they should. As a manager, you have the ability to grant people time to work on things. Be as generous with that gift as you can be. Give your people the room to do the culture work, and run interference for them if people higher up start to lean on them. Remember, the work of figuring out how the culture is getting in the way of individual and organizational success is going to take time—meetings, conversations, data analysis. Give them the time to do this work.

This, by the way, is why you really need a clear culture management system (see 8.1 above) with the support of senior management in place. Sometimes you'll want to play that card if you get push back from your supervisors. And HR should be able to help you with some ROI arguments when the top worries about how much time is being dedicated to your initiatives (remember what we said about the costs associated with wasted time and inefficiency?).

Tip 3 **HELP HR WITH THE METRICS**

If HR is helping you with ROI arguments, you can return the favor by helping them with metrics. Culture management requires good metrics, and as middle management, you are not only closer to the work, but you are often more cognizant of where processes are getting stuck or breaking down. That means you can be very helpful in developing the "in process" metrics that we talked about in Chapter 2 (2.5 Don't Forget to Measure Your Change Efforts).

8.5 What People Not in Charge Need to Know About Engagement

We are frequently asked a variation of this question: "What do you do if you want change, but the bosses don't get it?" When you're among the many people who are not in charge, pushing for change often feels like a distinctly uphill battle against forces that don't "get it." Of course, you don't have unlimited resources and power to enact change, so ignore the parts you can't control and focus on using the power you have. Here's some advice:

Tip 1 **PROCEED UNTIL APPREHENDED**

If you lack power but want to change culture, then one option is to take initiative and start changing things on your own. This phrase was Florence Nightingale's mantra, and it's obviously about not asking for permission. But what we like about her message is the reminder that you WILL be apprehended at some point, and that's when it is critical to be able show some results of your actions. The higher ups love results. So don't just "proceed" randomly. When you're moving in a new direction, develop some short-term experiments that are designed to show results quickly. Think of it as a pilot project. You probably already have the leeway to run a small pilot project. Be clear and intentional about it, so when someone does approach you with questions as to why you are doing something in a new way (i.e., you are "apprehended"), you'll have a good argument for why you did it.

Tip 2 **SHOW THAT YOU "GET IT"**

As frustrating as it can be when "the powers that be" don't "get it," you'd be surprised at how much they think you don't get it. There is almost always a communication gap between the top and bottom, so any way you can bridge that gap will support your culture work from the bottom of the pyramid. Share your opinions in meetings. Write on the internal blog. Leverage your network to get introductions and hopefully meetings with more senior people. If they have zero data about you, they'll do what everyone does: They'll make up a story about what you know, what you can do, and what you want, which can result in misguided or even counterproductive initiatives.

Tip 3 **BE PREPARED TO MOVE ON**

We're not trying to be negative with this one, but the truth is, sometimes the organization that you're working for is never going to create a position or a culture that will enable you to fulfill your destiny. With the tools we have provided in this book, you will be able to evaluate whether or not the change you are looking for is realistic at your organization. Life is too short to work for organizations that are not aligned with your personal success drivers—and in the long-term, forcing that route will be a lose-lose situation for both you and your bosses.

The Holy Grail of Stewardship

With the tools in this book, ideally, it will be easier to secure the resources to set up a Culture Team to act as a steward of the culture management system.

Culture work requires continuous attention. Depending on your organization, you may be the first person to draw attention to the importance of culture in driving engagement.

It is important to remember that your culture is like a garden—you can't leave it alone for too long. It requires constant tending and nurturing.

Sometimes this means small efforts, like watering or pruning a few branches on a daily basis, and sometimes it's bigger things, like ripping out entire bushes or creating an entirely new flower bed. Either way, the work is continuous.

That kind of work requires stewardship, and the perfect stewards are those who have the time, skills, and mindset to ensure that culture work moves forward at a steady pace. Here are some examples of how to do this.

Stewardship Play #1 **CREATE A CULTURE TEAM**

When we start working with an organization, one of the first things we do is set up a Culture Team.

SAMPLE CULTURE TEAM CHARTER:

Use this template as a starting point for defining how your culture team will work.

The Culture Team's roles can vary, but they include tasks like overseeing the culture assessments, developing and writing up culture priorities, helping to define culture metrics, and providing guidance on the development and implementation of the culture plays in the playbook.

Ideally the team has both horizontal and vertical diversity. You want to appoint people from as many departments or functions as possible to this team, because during their culture work, they will want to reach out to their peers, and you want as much of the organization covered in that process. You will also want representation from all the levels—including the senior management team—so all those perspectives are captured. Above all, whoever you appoint to the team must have a passion for doing culture work. You should never force someone to be on your Culture Team.

Stewardship Play #2 **CREATE A CULTURE "DESIGNATION"**

One of the organizations we studied in *When Millennials Take Over* went beyond creating a specific cross-functional team on culture. They started looking throughout the organization for the individuals (at all levels) who consistently demonstrated both knowledge and behavior that supported the growth and development of the culture. Those that did it the best— about 5% of their staff—were given the designation of "mentor."

Mentors provided the rest of the organization with guidance on what to do and how to do things in ways that were consistent with the core principles and behaviors that they had identified as central to their culture. Mentors would meet regularly and receive training on the specific aspects of the culture that needed to be reinforced.

The goal here was to give employees accessible tools and regular guidance, and to make sure that they could not go too far in the organization without running into someone who reinforces the organization's culture and mission. That's stewardship.

 ## What's Next?

That's up to you, isn't it?

Our next (and final) chapter is our QuickStart Action Guide, so we do have some more guidance, but the next step is going to be yours.

Start making a list of things you'll do. We think we've given you ample resources and guidance in this book for you to start making a plan—whatever your role in the organization—to start aligning culture with success in order to improve engagement. Try to get better metrics. Redesign a process that currently sucks. Talk to leadership about it. Research technology tools that might improve things.

Whatever you do, do something. We hope this guide has given you some places to start.

CHAPTER SUMMARY:
THREE THINGS TO REMEMBER

→ Engagement can't be everyone's job, yet it doesn't seem to belong to any single individual or group either. Instead, there needs to be a system capacity for culture management.

→ Human Resources can lead this effort, starting by building out the structure and processes needed for culture management.

→ CEOs and managers have a very important and specific role to play. Oh yeah, and everyone else does, too. Don't let anyone off the hook and make expectations clear about how culture is connected to daily work and organizational success.

QuickStart
Action Guide

By now you should see the main challenge here: intentionally shaping your culture in ways that will increase success—both for the organization and your individual employees. If you can consistently do that, you will see engagement levels consistently rising. It can even create a bit of a flywheel effect—the increased engagement increases discretionary effort, which contributes to even more success.

And like anything that's worth doing, it's going to take a bit of work on your part. Think of it like maintaining a beautiful garden. The work will be continuous throughout the year, though not all-consuming, leaving you plenty of time for your other work. Some of the work will be oriented towards long-term infrastructure and foundation, and some of the work will be more like maintenance—short term and fairly easy to handle. Here's our advice on both fronts.

FOUNDATION

For this to work over the long term, culture needs consistent attention inside your organization. Here's where you can start:

→ **Set up your baseline culture analytics as soon as possible.** The path to engagement ALWAYS starts with a crystal-clear picture of what your culture actually is. The longer you wait to provide that, the longer the whole process will take. If you don't have the resources to run a full culture assessment, you can at the very least engage in a quick qualitative study through interviews and focus groups.

→ **Create a home for culture in your organization.** Many organizations are either re-naming Human Resources entirely (we see more Chief People and Culture Officers these days), or at least creating a division of HR that is expressly focused on culture. If you're not large enough to have that structure (or can't make it happen with your leadership), then at least create an internal Culture Team that can carry the work forward.

→ **Articulate your success drivers.** At the heart of engagement lies people in your organization being successful, yet most people remain fairly superficial in their understanding of what drives success in their organization. Get together with others and try to flesh this out. You'll need some deep clarity here to make the long-term culture and engagement work successful.

MAINTENANCE

Don't overlook opportunities for some easy and quick wins that will signal to others in the organization that culture and engagement are about to receive more attention than they did in the past. Here's where you could start:

→ **Make your core values language more specific (and helpful).** Core values are a good place to start, but it would help if they are more specific, tied directly to what makes people successful, and easily confirmed by observable behaviors. Re-write the core values document with that in mind and share it around for feedback.

→ **Experiment with some processes that you already control.** Improving engagement will require you to change the way you do some things (the plays in the playbook), but if you can't yet pull off a full-on culture change project, you can always start at the end and modify processes with an eye towards improving success. If you get enough good examples, it might help advance the broader conversation about culture change and engagement.

→ **Leverage free technology.** There are a lot of online tools that can be used to help align culture with what drives success, and most of them have a free or nearly free version. Want to experiment with more transparent communications? Maybe you can get the trial version of some of the tools out there. (Check out culturetools.net for examples.)

APPENDICES

APPENDIX A

Managing Engagement in a Multi-Generational Context

 A.1 **Are Generations Even Real? (Yes, and Here's Why)**

The topic of generations frustrates a lot of people. We get it. First, there is the incessant complaining about "kids these days," which for a good ten years now has been squarely focused on the Millennials (impatient! entitled! too many trophies!). Of course, a few decades earlier we freaked out about Generation X (cynical slackers!), and before that it was the Baby Boomers (long-haired hippy freaks!). We do this every 20 years. It's annoying, but we doubt it's going to change any time soon.

And there are many who believe the whole topic amounts to no more than inappropriate stereotyping. After all, how can you say that an entire generation thinks or behaves in a particular way? It can't be true. There are tens of millions of individuals in any given generation, and they are all unique individuals, right?

Well, the truth is a little more complex: Yes, every individual is unique, and yes, broad generalizations about large groups are valid. It's a both-and. Think about it: We have no problem accepting that there are sociologically driven differences between men and women. We see different patterns of behaviors, approaches, etc., and there are researchers and academics in gender studies departments that can explain the why and how. Yet we also know that not all women (or men) are the same. If we can find value in looking at gender-based behavior, then we can do the same with generations.

It would actually help if we dug a little into generational theory. The generational researchers we trust the most are William Strauss and Neil Howe. Their book, *Generations*, explains how generations are formed, and even tracks them in the United States as far back as the early 1600s. They studied major trends and transitions in U.S. history, and they saw a pattern: Every thirty or forty years, there was a big transition associated with an interesting combination of forces/dynamics that they call "social moments." The Depression and World War II were social moments as were "the 1960s."

GENERATIONS: THE HISTORY OF AMERICA'S FUTURE

By William Strauss and Neil Howe (New York: William Morrow and Company, 1991), this is the seminal book we recommend for understanding generational theory.

These social moments shaped those who grew up in them, forming a generation with a set of values and behaviors that is uniquely different from that of those that came before or after them. In other words, the Baby Boomers, who grew up in the sixties, are noticeably different than Generation X, who grew up in the aftermath of the cultural shifts brought about in the sixties. And the Millennials are different still, having grown up in a social moment that is yet to be named (because we're still in the middle of it).

So why does any of this matter to employee engagement? Because generational differences seem to show up most strongly in the workplace.

When a new generation enters the workforce, it's not just that they feel the need to tweak things around the edges—it's that the whole system doesn't feel designed for them. Since almost every organization and industry has a multi-generational workforce, you must, at the very least, try to understand the different generations you have working for you.

The Three Generations in Today's Workforce

A.2

Workforces are typically made up of four generations, with a fifth right at the doorstep. The oldest generation is the "Silent Generation" (born between 1925 and 1942), but they are now just a sliver of the workforce, so we're leaving them off the list, and those from today's youngest generation (the one that comes after Millennials, who are still unnamed) are barely old enough to work. We're focusing on the three generations that are dominant right now: Baby Boomers, Generation X, and Millennials.

ONLINE TRAINING: MANAGING GENERATIONS IN THE WORKPLACE

A full eight-hour, on-demand practical and theory-based generational management training course.

BABY BOOMERS

Baby Boomers were born between 1943 and 1960 (yes, we know those are not the years you usually hear), so they are heavily represented in senior management at this point.[11] They grew up in a time of idealistic social revolution, with a can-do spirit: We came out of the second World War a global power, put a man on the moon, and enacted the first comprehensive policies to fight poverty and bring about racial equality. It was a time of movements and causes and collective action, and there was a sense that anything was possible. Thus as a generation, Boomers have always been very team/group focused and value hard work (often in the form of long hours), particularly when it is for a cause or a movement. They like stretch goals and believe success starts with "showing up." They were the first generation to really focus on efforts like "team building" in the workplace, but they are also known for sweeping conflict under the rug (when you're pursuing a cause, you don't want to seem splintered).[12]

GENERATION X

When Generation X hit the workforce in the 1990s, they were dubbed "cynical slackers." They are not, of course, slackers, but the cynicism is real. Gen X was born between 1961 and 1981, and growing up in the aftermath of the Sixties, they continuously experienced a set of "broken promises" laid out by their idealistic elders. Gen Xers grew up in a society thinking that large, gas-guzzling cars would be just fine, and then the oil crisis came along to counter that idea. Nuclear energy was then posed as a great fossil-fuel alternative, but then the crisis at 3-Mile Island proved it might not be the savior we thought it was. Even social institutions like marriage turned out to be less stable than we were told (divorce rates skyrocketed during this era). So cynicism is real for Gen X. As a result, they often look for "proof" to back up the words people use, and they are hesitant to trust someone based on titles or words alone: They look to your behaviors. The children of a generation of workaholics, they came home from school to an empty house (they were called "latch-key kids"), so they are known for being independent and adaptable, and as they developed in their careers, they were the first generation to advocate for work/life balance.

MILLENNIALS

The largest generation at 100 million strong, Millennials tend to be characterized as empowered and optimistic. Born between 1982 and 2004, material abundance, cultural diversity, and the connectivity of the digital age shaped their worldview and values. The internet gave them incredible power to connect, learn, and create.

There are more 11-year-old business owners in the Millennial generation, for example, than any other previous generation (and we don't mean lemonade stands—we mean profit-and-loss businesses). That means they show up in the workplace expecting to do things—to take action, move projects forward, and run experiments.

They had that power as children thanks to the internet, so they expected nothing less as entry-level employees. The abundance and diversity they grew up with means they are used to resources being available, and they are used to working with people from different skill levels, age groups, backgrounds on projects. That means they expect to work with people from different departments and different levels of seniority, and to try new and novel approaches to the situations they face, inspired by solutions they find in the office or an article they read online. Oh, and the notion that Millennials have been spoiled with trophies just for participating? That misses the point, actually. The attention we paid to Millennial children wasn't about spoiling them—it was about elevating their status in their homes and in society. Where previous generations pretty much ignored children's opinions on adult matters, Millennial children grew up in a time where adults engaged with them differently—negotiating with them, solving problems with them, and even interacting with them on a first-name basis. So even when they were young and powerless, they expected to have access and influence over those with more power than them. That same pattern is visible in the workplace. Millennials understand organizational hierarchy, but they also feel like they deserve a seat at the table.

Engaging Different Generations Differently

So what does all that mean for employee engagement? Well, remember that engagement is fundamentally about aligning what makes your organization successful with what makes your individual employees successful.

Clearly, each of the three generations will show up in the workplace with different approaches and expectations. But that doesn't mean we need to pander to those differences.

Generation X is known for being independent, so should you make sure that all your Gen X employees work alone and not on teams? Of course not.

Remember, organizations don't "engage" their employees the way that transitive verb implies. Engagement is a result of a culture aligned with individual and organizational success, so even thinking about this in terms of "engaging different generations differently" is misleading. Instead, we should be constantly analyzing the ways in which generational differences inside the organization might be impacting everyone's success.

For instance, take a good, hard look at some of the core processes in your organization, like the way you do staff/team meetings or performance reviews. It's quite likely that when those processes were invented, the generational makeup of your organization was different than it is today, and whoever was in charge back then likely designed the processes around their own approach and bias. In other words, your processes are not optimal for a multi-generation workplace.

When Millennials show up to a staff meeting and hear four or five managers report out on what they've been doing over the last week, they'll be perplexed. Why wasn't that shared via Slack or posted onto the shared drive? Why would we need to attend a meeting to share basic information with each other? And why is it always the managers leading the meetings? To a Millennial, these practices result in a lot of wasted time that could have been avoided by a more sensible use of technology and clearer purposes for the meetings themselves.

This doesn't mean you have to turn around and do your meetings the way Millennials want them.

Millennials are providing excellent data about what is currently working and not working. In the end, your processes should probably be constantly evolving just like the composition of your workforce is.

If you're not evaluating processes like that to determine whether they are making everyone more successful, and then you are sowing the seeds of disengagement.

Another area where generational differences will impact success is conflict resolution. The inability to identify, confront, and resolve conflicts inside organizations is one of the biggest inhibitors of success. We have seen that play out in organizations of all sizes, in just about every industry, and frequently generational differences can be at the heart of these conflicts. For example, a classic generational conflict has a Boomer manager complaining that her Gen X report is not a "team player," while at the same time the Gen X report is complaining that the Boomer is a micromanager. The source of the conflict lies in the way they interpret the same behaviors in very different ways—Boomers expect collaboration as the norm, where Xers are used to more independence in their work. Neither side is "right" here, and in the end they will need to negotiate a clear agreement about what kind of supervision and reporting is acceptable to both parties. When you know the generational differences and patterns well, it will actually help you get below the surface arguments of "team player" and "micromanager" and down into the behaviors that contribute directly to a successful working relationship.

A.4 Amplifying Your Generational Radar

Understanding generational differences helps you identify problems related to engagement and success drivers before they become too difficult to solve.

Even in the conflict example above, if the manager and direct report were each aware of the generational stereotypes, they probably would have known to address the team player and micromanaging issues earlier.

It's not that the Gen X employee would say, "Hey, you're a Boomer, so obviously you feel more comfortable when we all do work together in the same space, but I'm Gen X, so I like to be left alone." (Seriously, please don't ever say stuff like that.) But awareness of the pattern might prompt some more appropriate questions earlier on in the conflict ("So I'm noticing that we're scheduling a lot of group meetings about this, and to be honest, I think I get more done when we work in parallel...can we discuss our approach?"). You never really mention the Generations, but you use the knowledge to guide the conversation towards better problem solving. For example, the Gen X employee might end up providing more continuous updates to the manager, but via technology rather than in-person meetings, and the Boomer manager might fine-tune her agendas to ensure that the group meetings actually require everyone's perspective, in person. Addressing the conflict earlier always makes it easier. But processes and conflict are not the only areas where a stronger generational radar would benefit success and engagement.

MANAGING CONFLICT WITH CONFIDENCE:

A brief course about how to turn workplace conflict into an engine for growth and innovation.

ADJUST YOUR STRATEGY AND OPERATIONS

Pay attention to generational shift and how that is impacting your operating environment. In the world of franchising, for example, more and more franchise-based organizations are rethinking some core tenets of their business models. Millennials are starting to hit the age where they would be getting in as franchise owners, but as franchise expert Dr. Ben Litalien said during a presentation to a group of franchisees, "To a lot of Millennials, the franchising model looks a lot more like indentured servitude than a cool opportunity to run a business." So franchisors are looking into ways to give franchisees more flexibility and control. Hotel chains are also rethinking how they design their hotel lobbies to include more work tables and desks (with lots of plugs for charging!) to accommodate Millennials who want to work and play more collaboratively in those spaces rather than work alone in their hotel rooms. (We discuss office space directly in Chapter 6.) These small changes go a long way in serving generational priorities directly.

The rise of remote working is another indication of the way the workplace is adjusting for Millennials and causing discomfort for other generations. For Boomers in particular, success is about "showing up," so there is frequently an underlying and unspoken assumption that if I can't see you, you're not working. Instead of leaving all this unspoken, you will want to manage it directly, which may include setting clear standards for the frequency of communication among remote employees or establishing more detailed processes for managing accountability and tracking progress and results so that everyone feels like they are being held to the same productivity standards.

BROADEN YOUR CONCEPT OF PROFESSIONAL DEVELOPMENT

Traditional models of professional development have always focused on training and conferences. Larger organizations might add shadow assignments and mentoring, and pretty much all organizations allocate the lion's share of their investments in professional development for the senior staff—"What if we invest in our junior people, and then they leave?" (Though we always counter that with, "What if you don't invest in them—and they stay?") But the way the younger generation is consuming education is changing. There are a lot more bite-sized parcels of content being delivered, with more of it happening online or via mobile devices. Forcing younger generations into a previous generation's model of "training," may not work anymore. With a multi-generational workforce, you're likely to have to change some of your policies and the overall parameters of your professional development program to make it easier for everyone in your organization to start learning more quickly and more frequently.

And Another Thing: Engagement and Job Hopping

Speaking of data, it's incredibly important to bring as much of it as you can into your conversations about the connection between engagement and generational differences. Though equally important is making the distinction between which numbers help you draw effective conclusions and which numbers actually lead you astray.

A case in point is a commonly misinterpreted fact about Millennials: They are "job hoppers," which many equate with low engagement. We find nearly universal agreement from managers (anecdotally) when we talk to them—Millennials are hard to retain. And there are numbers to back it up (sort of). Gallup tells us that 21% of Millennials say they changed jobs in the previous year, compared to only 7% for the rest of the population. They are quick to point out that this Millennial turnover costs "the economy" $30 billion.[13]

First of all, don't get us started on the $30 billion figure—instead let's focus on the 21% figure compared to 7%. We are completely confident that their survey numbers are accurate (this is Gallup, after all), but here's the thing...

The numbers miss a hugely important factor: life stages.

Millennials are young, and you know what young people have always done? Hopped between jobs. If you look at the Bureau of Labor Statistics, you'll see that employees aged 20-24 had an average job tenure of only 1.3 years in 2014. But in 1998, it was even lower (1.1), and way back in 1983 it was only slightly higher at 1.5. And if you look at the next age bracket (25-34), the job tenure in 2014 (which would basically be all Millennials) was the same (3.0) as it was back in 1983 (all Boomers).

So contrary to popular belief, Millennial behavior is actually quite normal. Embrace this instead of trying to change it. Yes, we said embrace it! Fighting against this life-stage pattern is unlikely to yield results, but what if you changed your stance toward the Millennials who are leaving your organization? When your Millennials leave, are you staying in touch? Are you treating them like valuable "alumni," or are you resentful that they left? If you maintain a positive relationship, you could end up learning new things after they leave (even about your competitors), and they may come back to you later, equipped with new skills and knowledge.[14]

ABSTRACT AND SAMPLE CHAPTER,
***WHEN MILLENNIALS TAKE OVER* (2015)**

For further reading about generational differences
in the workplace, look no further than our book,
where we dig deep into all of this stuff.

 What Comes Next?

Just when you think you've got the Millennials figured
out, we're already seeing articles talking about the next
generation on the horizon. Like much of the writing on
generations, however, many of these articles lack a solid
theoretical foundation. A lot of writers are highlighting
the difference between what they call Generation Z
and the Millennials, but if you look more closely, they
are really highlighting differences between younger
Millennials (born between 1995 and 2004) and older
Millennials (born between 1982 and 1995). There are, in
fact, big differences between those two groups. That's
true for every generation, actually—the first half is always
somewhat different than the second half. But from a big
picture view, they are still part of the same generation.

In a Harvard Business Review article back in 2007, theorists Strauss and Howe actually gave a name to the generation following the Millennials: Homelanders.[15] At that time, the Homelanders were all still in diapers, so their assertion was not based on survey research, but on their historical trend analysis. They were predicting a shift—away from the Millennial focus on optimism and empowerment, and towards a more inward-focus on security and protection. At this point, some of those Homelanders are starting to enter the workforce. We think it will be several years before a clear picture of how this new generation will shake things up will emerge, but we are 100% certain that they will, in fact, shake things up.

Which brings us to the ultimate lesson around generations and employee engagement: The change is constant. You're never going to fully "figure things out," so your job, as we've explained above in this Appendix, is to amplify your generational radar, educate yourself on the differences and how they are showing up, and strategically apply that knowledge in your culture management activities. Your goal here is to create a workplace where every generation can be successful.

APPENDIX B

GLOSSARY: Definitions of Terms Used in This Book

The lessons in this book center around several key concepts listed below. As you now know, we choose our words carefully. Pay close attention to these definitions and how they are different to how others might describe culture and its components and attributes. Use them in YOUR culture work.

BABY BOOM GENERATION

The cohort of people born in the United States between 1943 and 1960, known for their idealism, group/team focus, and putting in long hours for "the cause."

CONTEMPORARY

A term we use in our culture model that refers to cultures and organizations that have worked to evolve their management practices to move beyond the traditional practices of the twentieth century, but have not quite pushed the envelope to be aligned with what we are now seeing as the "future of work." They have started to embrace ideas that are gaining popular acceptance these days, like experimentation, sharing information across silo lines, investing in professional development for employees, keeping updated on new technology, valuing diversity, promoting internal collaboration, and focusing on customer service. But they still haven't strayed too far from the roots of traditional management, so the advances they make in areas like transparency, agility, or innovation are limited.

CULTURE

Culture is the collection of words, actions, thoughts, and "stuff" that clarifies and reinforces what is truly valued in an organization.

CULTURE MANAGEMENT

Culture management is a system of activities, processes, and technologies that an organization uses to understand, shape, and change its workplace culture on an ongoing basis.

CULTURE PLAY

A culture "play" is an action that you take in order to change (or reinforce) the way you do things in your organization that is intentionally designed to move your culture in the direction of the culture priorities you have identified.

CULTURE PLAYBOOK

A Culture Playbook is a collection of Culture Plays, organized in a way that makes sense to the organization. Every Culture Playbook will have plays related to, for example:

→ Rituals and Artifacts

→ Stewardship

→ Talent/HR

→ Process

→ Structure/Design

→ Technology

The Playbook can be organized by these themes, or by level of effort, or by timeframe to implement, or as a sprint backlog (ongoing list of action items to be prioritized on a regular basis). A Culture Playbook should always be a living, breathing document, with new plays added on a regular basis—not a binder gathering dust on the proverbial shelf.

CULTURE STEWARDSHIP

The nurturing and development of processes or structures inside your organization to do the work of intentionally shaping and growing your workplace culture. This could include cross-functional culture teams or annual processes where culture is evaluated and changed.

CULTURE TEAM

A culture team is an internal group, typically drawn from multiple departments and multiple layers in the hierarchy, who is designated to support an organization's culture management efforts.

GENERATION X

The cohort of people born in the United States between 1961 and 1981, known for their independence, adaptability, skepticism (even cynicism).

"GOOD" CULTURE

A good culture is one where what is valued is aligned with what drives success.

EMPLOYEE ENGAGEMENT

Employee engagement is the level of emotional commitment and connection employees have to an organization, which is driven by how successful they are at work, both personally and organizationally.

FUTURIST

A term we use in our culture model, referring to cultures that are consistent with organizations that have transformed their management practices in ways that are setting the standards for where we are headed in the future of work. In short, they are more human-centric. They favor concepts like a rigorous focus on users, both internally and externally; constant innovation and improvement; extensive transparency to enable better decision making; fluid and flexible hierarchies; and systems of trust that unleash surprising speed and agility. The case studies from our book, *When*

Millennials Take Over, are good examples of futurist cultures, but we've seen others in our consulting work as well.

MILLENNIAL GENERATION

The cohort of people born in the United States between 1982 and 2004, shaped heavily by the social internet, abundance, diversity, and the elevated status of children, and known for feeling empowered and having higher expectations, particularly around culture.

SILENT GENERATION

The cohort of people born in the United States between 1925 and 1942, known for their work ethic, desire for stability, and embrace of command and control systems.

TRADITIONALIST

A term we use in our culture model for management practices that are more aligned with traditional management, that is ones that embrace the command-and-control approach that was established and perfected during the twentieth century. They tend to favor concepts like privacy, exclusivity, risk aversion,

predictability, slow-and-steady, measured change
with heavy change management, and emphasis on the
corporation rather than the individual.

Learn more at humanworkplaces.net.

Endnotes

1 Andrew J. Sherman, *The Crisis of Disengagement: How Apathy, Complacency, and Selfishness Are Destroying Today's Workplace* (Advantage, 2016), p. 25.

2 https://teamqli.com/stories/qli-voted-omahas-best-place-to-work/

3 http://www.netpromotersystem.com/about/employee-engagement.aspx

4 http://michael-roberto.blogspot.com/2013/01/lessons-from-challenger-accident.html

5 The Workplace Genome is a registered trademark of WorkXO LLC and QuestionPro Inc.

6 https://en.wikipedia.org/wiki/5_Whys

7 https://www.scrum.org/resources/what-is-a-product-backlog

8 Catherine Kendall, et al., "Group Projects with Millennials: The Question of Not Why...But How," *Journal of Learning in Higher Education*, Spring 2014 (Volume 10, Issue 1), pp. 53-58.

9 Both the anthropological research and Gore's application of it are covered in Malcolm Gladwell's, *The Tipping Point: How Little Things Can Make a Big Difference* (Boston, MA: Little, Brown & Company, 2000), pp. 177-86.

10 There is compelling research about the effects of financial incentives in Dan Pink's, *Drive: The Surprising Truth About What Motivates Us* (Riverhead Books, 2011).

11 Most sources refer to Boomers as those born between 1946 and 1964, since those years represent the start and end of the actual baby boom. But generations are based on what happened around you when you were coming of age—not how many babies were next to you in the maternity ward. Strauss and Howe's range starts at 1943 and ends at 1960 because those are the people who experienced "the sixties" and are more likely to have Baby Boomer values.

12 See Strauss and Howe's, *Generations* and Ron Zemke, Claire Raines, and Bob Filipczak's, *Generations at Work: Managing the Clash of Veterans, Boomers, Xers, and Nexters in Your Workplace* (New York: Amacom, 2000).

13 http://news.gallup.com/businessjournal/191459/millennials-job-hopping-generation.aspx?g_source=link_newsv9&g_campaign=item_221024&g_medium=copy

14 Andrew J. Sherman, *The Crisis of Disengagement: How Apathy, Complacency, and Selfishness Are Destroying Today's Workplace.* (Advantage, 2016), p. 25.

15 Neil Howe and William Strauss, "The Next 20 Years: How Customer and Workforce Attitudes Will Evolve," *Harvard Business Review* (July-August 2007).

Index